HUMAN RIGHTS

About the Author

Rev. M. Stephen is writer, author and theological teacher. He teaches theology and ethics at Faith Theological Seminary, Manakala, Adoor, Kerala. He received his M.A. from Kerala University; M.Th. from Serampore University and did his Doctoral Studies at Dharmaram Vidya Kshetram, Bangalore. He is author of several books and articles both in English and Malayalam. His well known books include 'A Liberated Vision' and 'A New Mission Agenda' published by ISPCK, Delhi.

HUMAN RIGHTS
Concepts and Perspectives

REV. M. STEPHEN
Faith Theological Seminary,
Manakala, Adoor
Kerala

CONCEPT PUBLISHING COMPANY, NEW DELHI-110059

ISBN 81-7022-956-1

First Published 2002

Published and Printed by
Ashok Kumar Mittal
Concept Publishing Company
A/15-16, Commercial Block, Mohan Garden
New Delhi-110059 (India)

Phones: 5648039, 5649024
Fax: 091–(11)–5648053
E-mail: publishing@conceptpub.com

PREFACE

Rights are the essential element of all creatures including human beings. Dictum of Lenin 'live and let live' is significant over here. Human rights play a very dominant role in the process of humanization. Recognizing the rights of others is integral to our spirituality. The perspectives like "all for one and one for all" and "unto the last" (John Ruskin), *Sarvodaya* (welfare of all) by Gandhiji and the Biblical concept of Kingdom of God are quite related. Kingdom of God affirms the rights of all human beings. Bible stands for the rights of the last and the least, that is the rights of the marginated or the subaltern.

God has created everyone in this own image. The dignity and the status are the rights of each person. God hates those who deny the rights of the poor. The sense of human right inspires to provide what is due to every person. The sense of rights should be central to any person and community. The rights enable a society to be right.

The human rights are to be upheld by the church the Christian Community. All the religious and non-religious communities should stand for justice. Sense of justice should be the central concern of Christians. It is important to be committed for justice and for the cause of human rights. If there is no sense of justice, there is no love and peace. Justice upholds the rights and the fair relationship and it is against oppression. Justice and human rights are close friends and one cannot stand without the other. I hope that this book "Human Rights" may enable the readers to have a proper understanding of different rights.

Rev. M. Stephen
M.A., M.Th., Th.D.

Puthenparambil
Near Railway Station
Kottayam - 686001
Kerala, India.

Contents

1

HUMAN RIGHTS
Definition and Meaning

Human rights are integral to the concept of justice. Justice means fairness. Dealing fairly to a person is what justice is. There is upholding of rights if there is justice. For humanness justice is essential. The denial of justice is the denial of human rights. Human rights uphold the dignity and status of the persons. Human rights means the affirmation of a dignified life to each individual. It involves love, mercy, humanness and just relationship.

Human rights look for the sustenance of each person in dignity. It demands the holistic development of persons and communities. Human rights are denied to the marginated, so what is essential is the overall development of the subaltern groups. Human rights were denied to them which contribute to their present destiny. Development is not to cater to the wants of the dominant, but to cater to the need of the poor and their upliftment. It is human to safeguard the rights of the depressed. Development means the economic stability and the social mobility of the oppressed ones. The poor are to be assisted substantially to develop themselves.

There is a right to live. To live is to live with dignity. The oppressive structures do not permit anyone to live with dignity or to affirm the rights. The dominant forces try to dictate "human rights" from their own selfish and exploitative outlook. They behave like the custodians of the human rights, but attempts to undermine it. Their main aim is to exploit others and accumulate for their own benefits. This is true with colonizers. They tapped all the resources of the third world and claim that they are the upholders of human rights. Liberation is an important means to redeem the marginated from their inhumanity. It affirms life and rights. For the proper affirmation of human rights, the transformation of the structure is essential. The transformation in relationship is central to human rights.

The human rights is not rooted in mere Christian charity. Charity is used as a means to escape from the real challenge of human rights. Charity create dependence, but creating sense of rights bring freedom and independence. Charity is a peripheral attempt to a deal with poverty and it is not to uphold human rights. In the question of human rights, charity is superficial. If anyone understands charity as human rights or as justice it is a misconception.

According to Felix Wilfred, "human rights is a question of regulating right relationships in society among individuals or groups relationships — which are humanizing, and therefore fair and just" (George V. Lobo, *Human Rights in Indian Situation,* p.VI). In today's context human rights is quite related to the concept of development and also the environmental issues. Challenging the environmental rights is badly affecting the whole of creation, including human beings. Creating ecological issues is a violation of the rights of human beings. The rights of women is another important aspect of human rights. Dignity is their right. The liberation from the clutches of colonialism, socio-economic and political oppression and exploitation is the right of all human beings. So it is their right to challenge evil structure.

The conservative evangelicals do not have a positive attitude towards human rights. They do not take up the structural issues very seriously. This is also a traditional view of Christians. The Justice issues should be taken up by all Christians as their concern for human rights. Work for the restoration of human rights is a mission of the church. It is also the prime responsibility of the Christian community.

2

HISTORY OF THE DEVELOPMENT OF HUMAN RIGHTS

The human rights are asserted not automatically. It is the result of several struggles. The working class struggled for their wages and privileges, the poor masses claim them their right for food, shelter and employment, the women protested against patriarchy demanded their equal rights with men, and the indigenous peoples raised their voices to have rights over their territory/land.

Human rights are found in all cultures but in diverse forms. The Greeks and Romans have rooted their understanding on the natural law. Aristotle and several other philosophers of Greece accepted the disparity. Thrasymachus, a sophist, was holding the view that "just or right means nothing but what is the interest of the stronger party" (Kadankavil Thomas, *Ethical World,* p.7). For Aristotle, women, children and slaves are inferior beings and accepted these as natural hierarchical order. No revolutionary spirit is found in him. According to him, the male is by nature superior and the female inferior, so also the slave is inferior in status by nature. George Lobo describes, "The Greeks particularly Aristotle and the Stoics, developed a notion of the natural law, according to which, each being had its own inherent value. They created the ideal of democracy wherein the citizen had certain basic rights simply by being born into the society. However, the Stoics thought of humanity in hierarchical order. At the bottom were the slaves, then came children, then women and then at the top free male adults. Children and women had very limited rights, slaves none at all. In practice, democracy in Greece was built in favour of 10 per cent of the free population, and that too at the expense of 90 per cent of slaves" (*Human Rights in Indian Situation*, p.5).

The Romans gave utmost importance to law, law was not dealing everyone fairly. In their view also the women and slaves were inferior in status, and they did not have equal rights with men or with their masters (Lords). Fr. George Lobo states, "The greatest contribution of the Romans was the development of (civil) law, not only the particular laws of each nation, but the *ius gentium* or "common law of all humans" (*Commune Omnium Hominum ius*) as the third century jurist Gaius phrased it. Here indeed was the basis for claiming a right simply on the grounds of one's humanity which is common to all human beings. However, this again applied only to the higher classes of society" (*Ibid.*, p.6).

Besides the Graeco-Roman views on human rights, the Judeo-Christian perspective have a greater contribution on it. As God is the creator of all, everyone has to be treated equally. The basic thinking came from the understanding that "man is made in the image and likeness of God" (*Gen.* 1:27) that everyone is created in the same dignity and status. Justice is another important dimension in this respect. The Christian vision is formation of an egalitarian society where there should be equity.

The Anglo-Saxon contribution to human rights is also noticeable. The Magna Carta or great charter of Medieval England (1215) played a significant role in the development of human rights. Great charter of English personal and political liberty was obtained from King John. It was a feudal document conceding contain rights of barons in return for their obedience to the King. The petition of rights (1628) was to gain Parliament's independence from crown in England. The English Bill of Rights (1689) was formed when King James II dissolved the Parliament and fled from the Kingdom, a body of responsible people gathered to form a parliament and offered the throne to William and Mary, subject to conditions laid down in the Bill of Rights. According to them, the parliament was to be freely elected by the people, and was to enjoy complete freedom of speech unhindered by crown or court (George V. Lobo, *Human Rights in Indian Situation*, p.7).

The English Philosopher John Locke spoke about right of life, liberty and property, which became fundamental in US declaration in independence in 1776. There was also Bill of Rights of the Constitution of Virginia on 12 June 1776 which was largely drafted by George Mason. It goes as follows: "All men are by nature equally free and independent, and have certain inherent rights, of which, when they enter into a state of society, they cannot by any compact, deprive or divest their posterity; namely the enjoyment of life and liberty, with the means of acquiring and possessing property, and pursuing and obtaining happiness and safety. All power is vested in, and consequently derived from, the people" (Concilium, 1990/2, pp.16-17).

The French contribution towards human rights is quite noteworthy. It was based on the slogan 'Liberty, Fraternity and Equality'. The following is the French Constitution (Decreed by the National Constituent Assembly in the years 1789, 1790 and 1791).

Declaration of the Rights of Man and of the Citizen: The representatives of the French people, constituted in national assembly, considering ignorance, neglect or contempt of the rights of man to be the only causes of public misfortune and the corruption of governments, have resolved to lay down in a solemn declaration the natural, inviolable, legitimate and sacred rights of man, so that this declaration, constantly before all members of the social body, should remind them at all times of their rights and their duties; so that the acts of the legislative power and those of the executive power, which can always be compared with the aim of any political institution, may be all the more respected, so that the complaints of citizens, henceforth founded on simple and indisputable principles, should always centre on the upholding of the constitution and the common good. Consequently, the National Assembly declares and recognizes, in the presence and under the auspices of the Supreme Being, the following rights of man and the citizen:

(i) Men are born and remain free and equal in rights. Social distinctions can only be founded on general usefulness.

(ii) The aim of every political association is the preservation of the natural and inviolable rights of man. These rights are liberty, property, safety and resistance to oppression.

(iii) The principle of all sovereignty resides essentially in the nation. No body, no individual can exercise authority which does not derive expressly from it.

(iv) Liberty consists of being able to do anything which is not harmful to another person. Thus the exercise of the natural rights of every man is limited only by the need to ensure that other members of society enjoy these same rights. These limits can only be determined by law.

(v) The law only has the right to forbid actions harmful to society. Anything which is not forbidden by law cannot be prevented, and no one can be compelled to do what is not ordained by law.

(vi) The law is the expression of general will. All citizens have the right to work; personally or through their religion, towards its establishment. It must be the same for everyone, whether it protects or punishes. All citizens, being equal in its eyes, are equally admissible to all offices, posts and public employment, according to their abilities, and with no other distinction but that of their virtues and talents.

(vii) No man can be accused, arrested or detained except in cases determined by law and according to the forms which it has prescribed. Those who solicit, expedite, carry out or have carried out arbitrary orders must be punished; but any citizen legally arrested must obey immediately; any resistance makes him guilty.

(viii) The law should establish only strictly and obviously necessary penalties, and no one can be punished except by virtue of a law which has been established and promulgated before the offence, and legally applied.

(ix) Every man being presumed innocent until he has been declared guilty, if it is considered essential to arrest him, any unnecessary force to secure his person should be severely repressed by law.

(x) No one should be harassed, for his opinions, even religious opinions, provided that they do not disturb public order as established by law.

(xi) Freedom of thought and expression is one of the most precious rights of man. Every citizen can therefore speak, write and print freely, subject to the responsibility for the abuse of such liberty in cases determined by law.

(xii) A guarantee of the rights of man and of the citizen necessitates a public force. This force is therefore instituted for the advantage of all and not for the particular use of those to whom it is entrusted.

(xiii) For the maintenance of the public force and its administrative expenses, a common tax is necessary. It should be shared equally among all citizens in proportion to their means.

(xiv) All citizens have the right to ascertain, by themselves or through their representatives, the necessity of the public tax, to agree to it freely, to supervise its use and to determine its quota, its assessment, its payment and its duration.

(xv) Society has the right to call to account any public agent of its administration.

(xvi) Any society in which rights are not guaranteed and the division of powers is not laid down has no constitution.

(xvii) Property being an inviolable and sacred right, no one can be deprived of it, except when public necessity, legally established, clearly demands it, on condition of a fair and previously agreed indemnity.

(Concilium 1990/2, pp.3-5)

The United Nations Organization framed the universal declaration of Human Rights. In June 1946 the UN General Assembly recommended the formulation of an international Bill of Rights. The universal declaration of human rights was adopted on 10 December 1948. This day is observed as the human rights day. Following is the Universal Declaration of Human Rights of United Nations.

Universal Declaration of Human Rights of the U.N. Preamble

Whereas recognition of the inherent dignity and of the equal and inalienable rights of all members of the human family is the foundation of freedom, justice and peace in the world.

Whereas disregard and contempt for human rights have resulted in barbarous acts which have outraged the conscience of mankind, and the advent of a world in which human beings shall enjoy freedom of speech and belief and freedom from tear and want has been proclaimed as the highest aspiration of the common people.

Whereas it is essential, if man is not to be compelled to have recourse, as a last resort, to rebellion against tyranny and oppression, that human rights should be protected by the rule of law, whereas it is essential to promote the development of friendly relations between nations.

Whereas the peoples of the United Nations have in the Charter reaffirmed their faith in fundamental human rights, in the dignity and worth of the human person and in the equal rights of men and women, and have determined to promote social progress and better standards of life in larger freedom.

Whereas Member States have pledged themselves to achieve, in cooperation with the United Nations, the promotion of universal respect for and observance of human rights and fundamental freedom.

Whereas a common understanding of these rights and freedom is of the greatest importance for the full realisation of this pledge.

Now, therefore,

The General Assembly Proclaims

This Universal Declaration of human rights as a common standard of achievement for all peoples and nations, to the end that every individual and every organ of society, keeping this Declaration constantly in mind, shall strive by reaching and education to promote respect for these rights and freedom and by progressive measures, national and international, to secure their universal and effective recognition and observance, both among the peoples of Member States themselves and among the peoples of territories under their jurisdiction.

Art. 1 : All human beings are born free and equal in dignity and rights.

They are endowed with reason and conscience and should act towards one another in a spirit of brotherhood.

Art. 2 : Everyone is entitled to all the rights and freedoms set forth in this Declaration, without distinction of any kind, such as race, colour, sex, language, religion, political or other opinion, national or social origin, property, birth or other status.

Furthermore, no distinction shall be made on the basis of political, jurisdictional or international status of the country or territory to which a person belongs, whether it is independent, trust, no-self-governing or under any other limitation of sovereignty.

Art. 3 : Everyone has the right to life, liberty and security of person.

Art. 4 : No one shall be held in slavery or servitude; slavery and the slave trade shall be prohibited in all their forms.

Art. 5 : No one shall be subjected to torture or to cruel, inhuman or degrading treatment or punishment.

Art. 6 : Everyone has the right to recognition everywhere as a person before the law.

Art. 7 : All are equal before the law and are entitled without any discrimination to equal protection of the law. All are entitled to equal protection against any discrimination in violation of this Declaration and against any incitement to such discrimination.

Art. 8 : Everyone has the right to an effective remedy by the competent national tribunals for acts violating the fundamental rights granted him by the constitution or by law.

Art. 9 : No one shall be subjected to arbitrary arrest, detention or exile.

Art. 10 : Everyone is entitled in full liberty to a fair and public hearing by an independent and impartial tribunal, in the determination of his rights and obligations and of any criminal charge against him.

Art. 11 : (1) Everyone charged with a penal offence has the right to be presumed innocent until proved guilty according to law in a public trial at which he has had all the guarantees necessary for his defence.

(2) No one shall be held guilty of any penal offence on account of any act or omission which did not constitute a penal offence, under national or international law, at the time when it was committed. Nor shall a heavier penalty be imposed than the one that was applicable at the time the penal offence was committed.

Art. 12 : No one shall be subject to arbitrary interference with his privacy, family, home or correspondence, nor to attack upon his house and reputation. Everyone has the right to the protection of the law against such interference or attacks.

Art.13 : (1) Everyone has the right of freedom of movement and residence within the borders of each state.

(2) Everyone has the right to leave any country, including his own, and to return to his country.

Art. 14 : (1) Everyone has the right to seek and to enjoy in other countries asylum from persecution.

(2) The right may not be invoked in the case of prosecutions genuinely arising from non-political crimes or from acts contrary to the purposes and principles of the United Nations.

Art. 15 : (1) Everyone has the right to a nationality.

(2) No one shall be arbitrarily deprived of his nationality

nor denied the right to change his nationality.

Art. 16 : (1) Men and women of full age, without any limitations due to race, nationality or religion, have the right to marry and found a family. They are entitled to equal rights as to marriage, during marriage and at its dissolution.

(2) Marriage, shall be entered into only with the free and full consent of the intending spouses.

(3) The family is the natural and fundamental group unit of society and is entitled to protection by society and the State.

Art. 17: (1) Everyone has the right to own property alone as well as in association with others.

(2) No one shall be arbitrarily deprived of his property.

Art. 18 : Everyone has the right to freedom of thought, conscience and religion; this right includes freedom to change his religion or belief, and freedom, either alone or in community with others and in public or private, to manifest his religion or belief in teaching, practice, worship and observance.

Art. 19 : Everyone has the right to freedom of opinion and expression; this right includes freedom to hold opinions without inference and to seek, receive and impart information and ideas through any media and regardless of frontiers.

Art. 20 : (1) Everyone has the right to freedom of peaceful assembly and association.

(2) No one may be compelled to belong to an association.

Art. 21 : (1) Everyone has the right to take part in the government of his country, directly or through freely chosen representatives.

(2) Everyone has the right to equal access to public service in his country.

(3) The will of the people shall be the basis of the authority of Government in periodic and genuine elections which shall be by, universal and equal suffrage and shall be held by secret vote or by equivalent voting procedures.

Art. 22 : Everyone, as a member of society, has the right to social security and is entitled to realisation, through national effort and international co-operation and in accordance with the organisation and resource of each State, of the economic, social and cultural rights indispensable for his dignity and the free development of his personality.

Art. 23 : (1) Everyone has the right to work, to free choice of employment, to just and favourable conditions of work and to protection against unemployment.

(2) Everyone, without discrimination, has the right to equal pay, for equal work.

(3) Everyone who works has the right to just and favourable remuneration ensuring for himself and his family an existence worthy of human dignity, and supplemented, if necessary, by other means of social protection.

(4) Everyone has the right to form and to join trade unions for the protection of his interests.

Art. 24 : Everyone has the right to rest and leisure, including, reasonable limitation of working hours and periodic holidays with pay.

Art. 25 : (1) Everyone has the right to a standard of living adequate for the health and well being of himself and his family including food, clothing, housing and medical care and necessary social services, and the right to security in the event of unemployment, sickness, disability, widowhood, old age or other lack of livelihood and circumstances beyond his control.

(2) Motherhood and childhood are entitled to special care and assistance. All children, whether born in or out of wedlock, shall enjoy the same social protection.

Art. 26 : (1) Everyone has the right to education. Education shall be free, at least in the elementary and fundamental stages. Elementary education shall be compulsory. Technical and professional education shall be made generally available and higher education shall be equally accessible to all on the basis of merit.

(2) Education shall be directed to the full development of the human personality and to the strengthening of respect for human rights and fundamental freedoms. It shall promote understanding, tolerance and friendship among all nations, racial or religious groups, and shall further the activities of the United Nations for the maintenance of peace.

(3) Parents have a prior right to choose the kind of education that shall be given to their children.

Art. 27 : (1) Everyone has the right freely to participate in the cultural life of the community, to enjoy the arts and to share in scientific advancement and its benefits.

(2) Everyone has the right to the protection of the moral and material interests resulting from any scientific, literary or artistic production of which he is the author.

Art. 28 : Everyone is entitled to a social and international order in which the rights and freedoms set forth in this Declaration can be fully realised.

Art. 29 : (1) Everyone has duties to the community in which alone the free and full development of his personality is possible.

(2) In the exercise of his rights and freedoms, everyone shall be subject only to such limitations as are determined by law solely for the purpose of securing due recognition and respect for the rights and freedoms of others and of meeting the just requirements of morality, public order and the general welfare in a democratic society.

(3) These rights and freedoms may in no case be exercised contrary to the purposes and principles of the United Nations.

Art. 30 : Nothing in this Declaration may be interpreted as implying for any State, group or person any right to engage in any activity or to perform any act aimed at the destruction of any of the rights and freedoms set forth herein. (George V. Lobo, *Human Rights in Indian Situation*, pp.80-84; Concilium 1990/2).

The organized voice for human rights are only a modern development, though one can find the traces of the struggles for it in the earlier centuries. Human rights are not only a personal, but a structural issue. The struggles for the rights do not stop, but to continue till it reaches its goals.

3

HUMAN RIGHTS IN THE TEACHING OF THE CHURCH

Though systematic reflection on human rights is a later development, the sense of human rights was strongly found in the Christian tradition, especially in the teaching of the Church. Church father Tertullian declared that it is the fundamental human right, a privilege of nature, that all human beings should worship according to their conviction.

The 'Rerum Novarum' (new things) by Pope Leo XIII, 1891, May 15 was the Magna Charta of socio-economic reconstruction. It deals with the working class. This encyclical was proclamation of the fundamental conditions for justice in the economic and social situation of the time. It affirms peace, justice and dignity of the persons. Pope Leo XIII affirms the fundamental right of workers, the dignity of the worker and dignity of work. Work, for him, belongs to vocation of every person as he expresses and fulfils himself. Everyone has the right to exert oneself for the sake of procuring what is necessary for the various purposes of life, and first of all for self-preservation, says Pope Leo XIII (*Encyclical letter Centesimus Annus* by Pope John Paul II, pp.8-14).

Pope Leo XIII also deals with the right to property. Private property does not have absolute value in his views. He also advocates the workers' right to form association. He also suggested the right to the limitation of working hours and the right to legitimate rest and the right of children and women are to be treated differently with regard to the type and duration of work. He stressed the hygienic conditions of the work place. He stated that it is neither just nor human so to grind men down with excessive labour as to stupefy their minds and wear out their bodies. Pope Leo XIII asserted the right for just wage. In his view, every individual has a natural right to procure what is required to live; and the poor can procure that in no other way than by what they can earn through their work. Fair wages is the right of every individual. An individual also has the right to exercise his religious duties (*Ibid.*, pp.16-20).

Pope Pius XI was very conscious of human rights. He defended the rights of human beings for better social and economic conditions (Quandragesimo Anno, 1931). He also brings out the divine origin of human rights such as to live and enjoy bodily independence together with the means necessary for existence, the right strive to attain the ultimate end as determined by God, the right to association and to the ownership (Divini Redemptoris, 1937). Pope Pius XII denounced the violation of human rights and defended the cultural and political rights of all the citizens in his Christmas messages in the years 1942 and 1943 (George Lobo, *Church and Social Justice*, pp.80-83).

Another important document on human rights from the Catholic Church is the encyclical *Pacem in Terris* (peace on earth) by John XXIII, in 1963. According to this document man has universal inviolable and inalienable rights and duties. Everyone is to recognize and observe their mutual rights and duties. According to *Pacem in Terris* the rights are as follows :

1. Every man has the right to life and a worthy manner of living. This includes food, clothing, shelter, rest, medical care and necessary social services (right to security in cases of sickness, inability to work, widowhood, old age, unemployment, or in any other case in which he is deprived of the means of subsistence through no fault of his own).
2. Man has right pertaining to moral and cultural values, namely, rights to respect and good reputation; to freedom in searching for truth and in expressing his opinions, and in persuit of art; to truthful information; and share in the benefits of culture and, therefore, to basic education, technical and professional training, and even higher studies.
3. Every person possesses the right to worship God privately and publicly.
4. Human beings have the rights to choose freely their state of life—including religious vocations—and to establish a family with equal rights and duties for men and women.
5. Human persons have the right to free initiative and responsibility, to work, to proper working conditions, to just wages, and to private property even of productive goods. These are economic rights.
6. Every man has the right to assembly and association.
7. Every human being must also have the right to freedom to movement and of residence within the confines of his own country and if there is just reasons, the rights to emigrate to other countries and take up residence there.
8. There are political rights such as those of active participation in public affairs and of efficacious, impartial and just, juridical protection (John Descrochers, *The Social Teaching of the Church*, pp.125-127).

Vatican II : Gave utmost importance to human rights. They are as follows :

1. The basic equality of all must be recognized.
2. The exalted dignity is proper to human person, so his rights and duties are universal and inalienable. Food, clothing and shelter which help persons to be truly human must be made available to everyone.
3. The human persons must have the right to choose the state of life freely and to found a family, the right to education, to employment, to a good reputation, to respect, to appropriate information, to activities in accord with the norm of one's conscience, to protection of privacy and the rightful freedom in religious matters too.
4. All have the right to free assembly and association. Every form of discrimination, whether social or cultural, whether based on sex, race, colour, social condition, language or religion are to be overcome and eradicated as contrary to God's intent (George V. Lobo, *Church and Social Justice*, pp.89-97).
5. There is the right to life and dignity. This is usually violated by racism, caste prejudice or by torture. It is increasingly felt that capital punishment is barbaric and is not an adequate means of safeguarding the social order. It argues that every human being, even the child in the mothers womb, receives its right to life directly from God. So deliberate and direct disposing of an innocent life is condemned (George V. Lobo, *Christian Living According to Vatican II*, p.269).

The World Council of Churches is a strong voice of human rights in the world. It advocates for justice, peace and people's rights. It raises voice for social and racial justice. It combats racism as racism is a violation of human rights. The Fourth Assembly of W.C.C., Uppsala (Sweden) in 1968 realised the fact of inequality in economic status and discriminations on the basis of race, sex and class. The message of the Assembly was that we heard the cry of those who long for peace; of the hungry and exploited who demanded bread and justice; of the victims of discrimination who claim the human dignity; and of the increasing millions who seek for the meaning of life. The Uppsala Assembly sees the violation of human rights and the abuse of power everywhere.

World Council of Churches talk about people's rights, defending the rights and dignity of the fellow human beings. The Commission of the Churches on International Affairs (of W.C.C.) is having the following charges : (1) This Commission is charged to serve the nations by making a Christian witness on behalf of peace with justice and freedom. (2) Church is to work for the healing of nations. It is to see whether human rights are violated in the context of internal or international conflict of nations.

4

HUMAN RIGHT VIOLATIONS IN THE GLOBAL CONTEXT

The human right violations are taking place in the local and global context everyday. Those who are appearing as the defenders of human rights also act in a fascist way in order to violate human rights. Systemic violence is common in all context so also the human right violations. The human right violations are evident in the form of patriarchy, fascism, colonialism/imperialism and discriminations based on race class, caste or gender.

The western imperialism has contributed so much to global level human right violations. Mahathir Mohammed observed that, "perhaps the focus on human rights as being crystallised during the second world war. Prior to that, the Europeans, who has nicely divided up the world into their empires where they were free to do what they liked with their colonial inhabitants, did not believe in the universality of human rights. The rights of the white man were to rule the non-whites, to civilise them, and to spread their particular religion. This was the white man's burden and it was glorified as God given task" (*Human Wrongs*, p.5). For the last five hundred years the Europeans colonized the third world countries and tortured and killed millions of indigenous peoples. They coveted the land of the inhabitants of the third world. The economic exploitation and political oppressions are the forms of human right violations, which the westerners practiced everywhere. The neo-colonial structures are built up in order to have economic control over the third world countries by the western powers in the form of globalization. The multinational corporations and transnational corporations are the agents of neo-colonialism. According to Winin Pereira, the structures of injustice through which the west accomplished its earlier subordination of the rest of the world, have not been dismantled; in fact, they are now firmly enshrined in economic "laws". The so called international institutions including the UN and its progeny, the International Monetary Fund (IMF), the World Bank (WB) and the World Trade Organisation (WTO), that the west founded and vigorously supports are merely complex tools created by the west to implement its objectives even while disguising its selfish aims. These institutions act as surrogates for the west, being more effective because they are assumed to be neutral by their unexpecting and naïve victims" (*Inhuman Rights*, pp.3-4).

The west claims to be custodian of human rights, but actually it promotes violence and injustices. Winin Pereira brings to light the contradictory stance of the western world as follows : "Thus the west can maintain that it is fostering the right to life even while its economic programmes, imposed in the name of "development" impoverish and kill people. It claims to be spreading democracy, even while it supports tyrants in countries where it has large economic interest. It claims to abhor violence even while it sells arms which incites conflicts around the globe. It promotes the right to food even while its industrialised agricultural system is unsustainable, and it continues to use food as a weapon for further subjugation. It promotes the right to health even while the effluents of its industries poison people directly and are also responsible for the breakdown of the human immune and reproductive systems. And so it goes nearly every right that the west claims to promote is matched by actions that violate" (*Inhuman Rights,* p.4).

Millions and millions of indigenous peoples (roughly 90 millions) are eliminated by the western powers. The Maoris and other indigenous groups in Australia and Red Indians of United States are brutally killed by them for their selfish gains. According to Chandra Muzaffar, "It was western dominance which, through the brutal, barbaric slave trade robbed 25 million sons and daughters of Africa of their freedom and dignity (*Human Wrongs*, p.1).

The Second World War saw the tragic death of six million Jews in Germany by the brutal treatment of Adolf Hitler. It was a gross violation of human rights. Another devilish human rights violation was done by America on Hiroshima and Nagasaki where millions of Japanese were killed and their tragic suffering continue even today.

In the Vietnam war, there was bombing and killing of innocents, the same pattern was continued in Iraq. These are all the cruel acts of US and allies. In Bosnia-Herzegovina, Serbs butchered 200,000 Bosnian Muslims and Croats. 30 lakhs people becomes refugees and it was a severe brutality and bloodshed. The ethnic crisis contribute to human right violations in the form of genocide.

The economic blockade is imposed on third world is one of the inhuman methods used by the western countries in order to suffocate the people to death. The 'All India Anti-imperialist Forum' observes, "Ever since the second world war the US imperialists have been engaged in expanding the network of military bases to all corners of the world. To establish an unchallengeable supremacy they carried out military interventions imposed economic blockades and engineered local and partial wars. Other destructions and losses apart, the loss of human lives alone in these local and regional wars exposes the scale of imperialist brutality and savagery" (Declaration adopted by the Anti-Imperialist Convention Nov. 14-17, 1995, Calcutta, p.2). The economic blockade against Cuba, Iraq, Iran and Libya are the examples for this imperialism.

Human right violations are also found in the form of militarism. United States is having a foremost place in the sale of weapons to other countries to promote international conflicts. The military intervention in the name of protection and freedom is one of the cunning method used by western powers. It is observed that "development and stockpiling of nuclear and other lethal weapons of mass destruction by different imperialist powers is going on unchecked. Each military budget of the imperialist states recording steep rise. In the face of an unprecedented crisis of recession, militarization has become a general feature of economy in every capitalist-imperialist country" (Declaration adopted at the Anti-imperialist Convention, p.4). There are cases where the military also involve in the human rights abuse such as torturing the innocents and raping the women. The military sometimes act like a mad dog.

In the name of colour, the South African blacks and US minorities undergo several kinds of discriminations. Apartheid was used as an instrument to curtail the rights of the blacks. But after a long years of struggle their rights are attained. But they had to give several lives for their cause. They could overcome the unjust situations as they fought for human rights.

One of the significant human right violations is found from the Chinese side over against the peaceful Tibetans. The UN is not dared to question the injustice of China. In 1950, the Chinese soldiers crossed the border of Tibet. They demolished 6000 Tibetan Buddhist temples. They had to run for life to India as their culture and history was spoilt or destroyed by them. Tibetans work for human rights. The Sannyasins protest against Chinese aggression and brutality.

The Chinese try to chase away Tibetans as they became a minority. Only 60 lakh Tibetans left in Tibet. Chinese allowed 75 lakh Han people or race to occupy Tibet. The Tibetan Buddhist were beaten, strangled, shot, hanged, drowned and burned by Chinese since they did not renounce their religion. Many thousands of children were taken away from parents and never seen them again. Many men and women were sterilized in traditional ways.

International Commission on Jurists investigated the issue and said that the Chinese guilty of "the gravest crime of which any person or nation can be accused that is of genocide, the intent to destroy, in whole or part, a national, ethnical, racial or religious group as such".

When Chinese occupied Tibet it was reported to UN Assembly, but the request was shelved. But in 1959, the UN Assembly resolves:

(a) Tibetans have the right to civil and religious liberty.
(b) They should enjoy the autonomy.
(c) Fundamental human rights and freedom of the people are denied forcibly by Chinese. (The Dalai Lama. *My Land and My People,* New Delhi, Srishti Publishers, 1997, pp. 217-234).

The UN General Assembly in 1961 was gravely concerned of human rights violation in Tibet. But the UN failed to enforce the rights of Tibetans as it was intimidated to deal the issue with China. Here once again it is proved that the superpowers are above the human rights and they are in fact the champions of human rights abuse.

As the exploitation, injustices, various forms of discriminations, imperialistic interests and neo-colonialism continue the human rights violation is a fact in the world today.

5

HUMAN RIGHTS VIOLATION IN INDIA

A brief survey of human right violations in India will help to know what is happening in Indian continent. The Aryan invasion is primarily contributed to human rights violation in India. The Dravidians live in dignity and equality but the Aryans tried to subjugate them and to discriminate them. The Aryans claim their superiority over the Dravidians and the caste system was introduced as a way to dehumanize the Dravidians. Discrimination in the name of caste is the human rights violation as a systematic violence.

The *dalits* are treated as sub-humans by the dominant and they are oppressed. Their plight is the creation of the Brahminic class to exploit the resource and to enjoy the privileges. Felix Wilfred states, "The deep wound and pain suffered in the heart at the daily experience of humanity is echoed in the prayer of Kisan Phagu, a dalit poet: "Lord make one a beast or a bird but not Mahar". Denying the most basic right to be human persons is the most abominable crime of our society" (*Human Rights in Indian Situation*, p.VI). The *dalits* are curtailed of their privileges in all spheres of life. They are marginated from the main stream of the society.

The women also undergo several kinds of sufferings as violence against them. The patriarchal society does not recognize their equal status with men. It is male chauvinistic. The women are considered as objects and oppress them in the most inhuman way. They are alienated economically, politically and gender-wise. The *dalit* women are the most victimized women. Their alienation includes the social as they are discriminated on the basis of birth (caste). It should be noted that the issues of the *dalit* women are totally different from the elite woman. Elite women can be the instruments of violence against the *dalit* and the poor woman.

The dowry deaths are common in the Indian situation. Wife-beating, harassing and raping the women are very much found in our context. There are discriminations in the sphere of labour as they are less paid. The sexual exploitation in the workplace, in the centres of education and in the field of sports and games are also not uncommon. The domestic violence and violence from the society are very much part of human right violations.

The tribal people are demanding their territorial integrity and freedom. Their dignity is questioned and they are exploited. The resources are tapped. Politically they are powerless and economically marginated. Their active participation and recognition of their identity is not ensured. Their rights are denied. They are considered as illiterates and savages which dehumanize them. When they raise questions, they are suppressed by use of force. The *Adivasis* in different parts of our country are chased away from their hàbitat. The Narmada valley project has evacuated around 10 lakh *Adivasis*. In the name of development the human rights are violated. It is assumed that *Adivasis* have no ownership over the land which is a grave mistake. Though they have no documents they have right over the land. Their right to life depends on the land and forest. Government is one of the great instrument of human right violations in this regard. The *Adivasis* are tortured, their women are sexually exploited, their privileges are exploited. The law and order system also fail to listen when they cry for justice.

Human right violations are found at the time of emergency. The emergency was proclaimed on 25th June, 1975 which lasted for 19 months. There was suppression of civil liberties and abrogation of the rule of law. Several innocents were detained and were treated badly. M.M. Thomas observed that the detainees are not only denied access to the courts and there is also clear evidence that some are being tortured. There was no freedom of press, freedom of association and freedom of assembly. Most of the opposition leaders were arrested and put to jail without providing the legal or constitutional rights. Fundamental rights were violated. Imposing the 'Maintenance of Internal Security Act (MISA)', many were detained but not produced before the court. Some persons were disappeared and were found dead later as the police authorities evade any responsibility. (M.M. Thomas, *Response to Tyranny: Religion and Society*, Vol. XXIV, Nos.2 & 3, 1977).

The lock-up deaths are common in India today. Most of the victims are the poor. Violent means are used to prove the guilt of the suspect. Police is understood as the guardians of human rights, but they sometimes turned to be the tyrants who violate the human rights. Distorting the cases to save the culprits because of political pressure is also noted from the protectors of law and order.

In Indian situation poverty is the embodiment of dehumanization. Right to bread is the right of every person. But their human right is denied in India. More than 60 per cent of the people are living below the poverty line. The poverty deaths are not uncommon in our country. According to Moses P. Manohar, "Although a vast majority of the Indians live a poverty stricken life, there is no proper legal measure to protect them and no one seems to be serious about it. Poverty is accepted as 'natural'. Therefore, it is very essential to understand poverty as a human right violation. Poverty is not natural. It is the expression of many forms of human rights violation. At the outset poverty denies the right to life, which is the cardinal right" (*Poverty and Human Rights*, p.10).

In Orissa, especially in Kalahandi district there are cases of starvation deaths. In the tribal belts children and others usually die because of poverty. Starvation deaths are reported from Madhya Pradesh, Maharashtra, Bihar and even from Kerala which claimed to be literate and more developed compared to other states. The government authorities are closing their eyes to the stark realities of life. Bureaucracy is corrupt and they are irresponsible.

6

BIBLICAL INSIGHTS ON HUMAN RIGHTS

According to Eugene B. Borowitz, the Jewish equivalent of 'right' derives from the compelling Jewish response to God as the absolute 'owner' in the economic metaphor or 'King' in the related political usage or more directly as creator ("The Torah, Written and Oral, and Human Rights: Foundations and Deficiencies", Concilium, 1990/2, p.25). He continued to say that Judaism, asserts inalienable dignity inheres in every human being as God has created human beings in his own image. Judaism, he states, teaches that no one can ever take away from a human being an elemental value which God has bestowed upon everyone and which God never alienates (*Ibid.*, p.27).

The statement 'man is made in the image of God' (Gen. 1:27) is the affirmation that human beings have the dignity and right and the manipulation of one by another is never promoted. According to George Lobo, "Human dignity and human rights belong together. No human rights without human dignity; no human dignity without human rights". (*Human Rights in Indian Situation*, p.12). The Old Testament is very clear on the rights of the poor and the marginated.

Righteousness, Shalom and Justice ensure the right of the powerless. Sin brings the alienation, margination and human rights violation.

It is found in the form of structural evil. God reinstates the people of Israel from the bondage of Egypt which is the restoration of Human rights. They were oppressed and there were no economic or political rights for them. This plight was challenged by liberating the people of Israel from Egypt (Ex:3:7ff; 23:9). The Jubilee (Lev. 25) is the best example for the restoration of human rights. It indicates a transformation of relationships and affirms equity and justice. According to Elsa Tamez, "The oppressed and the poor suffer exploitation and death, both physical and psychological; they suffer discrimination and degradation. To speak of liberation, therefore, is to speak of the struggle of an oppressed people in quest of their rights and spurred on by the hope that the victory will be real because their God is at their side in the struggle" (*Bible of the Oppressed*, p.3).

The prophets of the Bible are the defenders of human rights. They question the oppression or tyranny of the powerful (Heb. 'anah') over the poor which degrade the human person. The systemic violence is quite found in the society where the dominant class control the system with selfish motives: overturning the justice, exploiting the poor, crushing the powerless and forcing the poor to be slaves without providing proper wages (Jere 7:1ff; Am 2:6-7; 4:1-11). The prophets were never silent over the human right violations, but vehemently criticized the representatives of injustice. They upheld the human rights as they upheld justice (Am.5:24).

The covenant law of Israel was concerned of the rights of slaves (Ex. 21:2-21). Gerhard Von Rad states that Old Testament covenant law is noted for its passionate interest for the poor, slaves and strangers and God of Israel watches particularly over the rights of the poor who have no property and to whom justice is denied. God defends the rights of widows, orphans, sojourners and poor (Zc 7:9-10; Dt. 24:17; Job. 24:9). Taking care of the welfare of the poor and safeguarding the marginated is the foremost concern found in both Old and New Testaments.

The New Testament is very aware of the human rights. The oppression of the dominant over the powerless is understood as violation of human rights as human dignity is denied. The unequal distribution of resources is also denial of human rights. Poverty is another example for the violation of human rights. In Jesus' time the Romans (imperial power) and Jewish (dominant/elite Jews) nexus controlled the structure and they oppressed the poor. Here Jesus was stating that Kingdom of God affirms the rights of the poor as it empowers them and restore their dignity. Kingdom of God upholds the dignity of persons, justice and righteousness. The right and dignity of all persons regardless of class, race and gender is upheld by the New Testament (Gal. 3:28). Galatians 3:28 (is usually referred as magna carta of freedom) and Luke 4:16-21 (the Nazareth manifesto) are the manifestoes of human rights.

Jesus was the Champion of human rights as he challenged the inhuman elements (Mt. 21:12-13). Jesus vision was socialistic. He recognized the dignity of all persons. He executed justice without any prejudice (Jn. 8:1ff). The right of the poor to gain their dignity was a great concern of Jesus. Rights of the marginated was understood by Jesus as the prime factor in human rights. As Jesus was siding the poor he was siding the human rights. As Jesus recognized poverty as injustice and an element of dehumanization, he reacted against the dominant class who were the instruments of oppression. The rich were criticized by Jesus as they were the agents of human right violations (Mt. 19:16-25; LK 12:14-21).

There was serious human right violations found in the Graeco-Roman context which is reflected in Acts of the Apostles and Pauline Corpus. The minority rights were very much curtailed. The Christian minority was persecuted by the Roman imperial power and other fanatics. The dominant religious communities attacked Christians. Religious freedom was not enjoyed by the Christians. The Roman authorities killed several of the Christians and their leaders without any cause. The rights were confined to the dominant class. Everyone was not Roman citizen, but Paul was a Roman citizen. He affirmed his rights as a Roman citizen as he responded to injustices (Acts 21:39; 22:25-30).

7

HUMAN RIGHTS AND RELIGIOUS TRADITIONS

The religious traditions have their own particular views regarding human rights. Hinduism mostly talk about dharma, especially the caste duty (*kuladharma*) which is nothing to do with human rights. It is, in fact, totally against human rights. The privileges are enjoyed by the upper castes and others are denied of their dignity and rights. Aryan scriptures (*Vedas*) describe about the dignity and privileges the Aryan men and women enjoy, but these scriptures are either silent over the condition of *Dalit* men and women or discriminatory over them. The caste hierarchy is to violate the human rights, since it creates margination-equal status was never upheld. According to George Lobo, "The *Dharmashastras* seek to protect the various customs and practices of people belonging to different castes, communities and professions. The emphasis is our duties, not on rights, as in most ancient societies. This could lead to the neglect of human rights in favour of maintaining a traditional social order" (*Human Rights in Indian Situation*, pp.22-23). Manusmriti also advocates the *varna* theory which dehumanizes humanity and it is quite male chauvinistic.

The manifestation of Hinduism is dominantly Aryanism. It is controlled by caste system so equality, love, mercy and justice are confined to the Brahmins and other upper castes and it never implied in relation to the dalits. The concept 'do not harm' or *Ahimsa* (non-violence) itself is a contradiction in this regard, as the *Shudras* and *Panchamas* are ill-treated and oppressed by the upper castes. Caste system itself is a violation of human rights. Ideologically and practically the Aryan principles undergo a severe crisis. The unitive vision, *advaita*, itself is contradictory, though it is a fascinating idea, because of the neglect of the poor on the basis of caste disparity. Though *karuna* (mercy), *tyaga* (renunciation), love and welfare of poor (God is *Deenabandhu*) is the concern of Indian Scriptures, it is not practiced seriously by Hinduism. As caste system was against human rights, Dr. Ambedkar and several others had a quest for an adequate religion rejecting Hindu religious traditions.

Jainism and Buddhism accept the dignity of human life and the right to life of all living beings. *Ahimsa* is the key idea in Jainism which condemns the killing or torturing any beings. Preservation of life and honouring life are significant in Jainsim. *Ahimsa* is linked to justice by Jainism—Justice in Rule and Justice in the community. *Ahimsa* is abstention from injury to living beings. The Jainist understanding of *Ahimsa* (non-violence), *satya* (abstention from telling lie), *Asteya* (abstention from stealing), *Brahmacharya* (abstention from sensuality in thought) and *Aparigraha* (non-possession) enable to an extent to have a sense of human rights (*Religious Traditions in India*, edited by P.S Daniel, David C. Scott and G.R. Singh, p.183). The concepts like absence of greed (*nirlobhata*), renunciation (*tyaga*) and compassion (*karuna*) are contributing to the understanding of human right or human dignity.

Buddhism is also a religion of non-violence (*Ahimsa*). It rejects the greed and recognizes the value of *tyaga* (renunciation) and *karuna* (mercy). The integrity of creation is upheld by Buddhism. The right to life is the essential teaching of it. Desire is understood as the cause of all sufferings so it teaches to overcome desire as a solution, which certainly is concerned of the welfare of all. Though the issue of human right is not explicitly dealt in traditional Buddhist teachings we can get clues from it. The modern Buddhism is quite aware of the issues like ecology, woman issues and human rights. According to the Dalai Lama, "The true expression of non-violence is compassion". He continued to say that "True compassion is universal in scope. It is accompanied by a feeling of responsibility. To act altruistically, concerned only for the welfare of others, with no selfish or ulterior motive, is to affirm a sense of universal responsibility". (H.H. the *Dalai Lama*, "Importance of Non-violence in the society", DRELOMA: *Drepung Loseling Magazine*, p.6).

The dignity of human beings is stressed by Islam as God 'breathed this spirit into man' (*Quran* 15:21). Freedom of conscience is respected by Islam. According to *Quran* "There shall be no compulsion in religion' (2:256). As in Biblical thought, in Islam God is the possessor of all things and man is only a steward. The concept of 'Zakat' is sharing of wealth to the poor, but it is reduced to be mere charity or alms giving. Roger Garaudy points out that on eight occasions (3:95; 4; 124; 13:23; 17:40; 40:40; 43:17, 48:6; 57: 18) the *Quran* reminds us that 'Allah makes no distinction between human beings, be they men or women' ("Human Rights in Islam: Foundation, Tradition, Violation" Concilium 1990/2, p.56). He states that *Quran* abolishes the hierarchy between man and woman instituting not only their 'equality' or their 'complementarity' but their 'Ontological unity': 'Your Lord created you from one single being' (4,1).

In the case of polygamy also justice is emphasized. It is permitted only if one could deal the woman justly. If it is not possible the men were urged to marry only one (4,3). It is observed that all kinds of segregation and subordination come from tradition and not from the message of the *Quran*. (*Ibid*., p.57). This is not quite true. The patriarchal elements are also strong in Islam as, according to Sharia, no woman may hold any public office which involves exercizing authority over man (*Quran* 4:34). *Quran* also disqualify the woman from being competent witness in serious criminal cases (2:282). These can be regarded as serious violation of women's right (Abdullahi Ahmed Al-Naim, "*Quran*, Sharia and Human Rights: Foundations, Deficiencies, Prospects", Concilium, 1990/2, p.63). Sharia guarantees only minimum rights to woman. According to Abdullahi Ahmed, Sharia violates the freedom of religion as it is a crime punishable by death for a Muslim to repudiate his faith in Islam (*Ibid*., p.64).

8

INDIAN CONSTITUTION AND HUMAN RIGHTS

The Indian Constitution which is the brain child of Dr. B.R. Ambedkar, the architect of Indian Constitution which came to final form in 1949. Democracy, socialism and secularism are the pillars of Indian Constitution. The fundamental rights are the core of Indian Constitution.

The Constitution classifies the Fundamental Rights under six groups as follows:

1. Right to equality;
2. Right to particular freedoms;
3. Right against exploitation;
4. Right to freedom of religion;
5. Cultural and educational rights;
6. Right to constitutional remedies.
   (See Chapter XII, 14)

Particular Fundamental Rights

1. Right to Equality

Art. 14 : "The State shall not deny to any person equality before the law or the equal protection of the laws within the territory of India". The first implies the absence of any special privilege in favour of any individual and the equal subjection of all to the ordinary law; the second implies equality of treatment in equal circumstances.

Art. 15 : (1) "The State shall not discriminate against any citizen on grounds of religion, race, caste, sex, place of birth or any of them".

(2) On such grounds, there should not be "any disability, liability, restriction or condition with regard to -

(a) access to shops, public restaurants, hotels and places of public entertainment; or
(b) the use of wells, tanks, bathing ghats, roads and places of public resort.

(3) and (4) Nothing in this article shall prevent the State from making any (special) provision for women and children; or "for the advancement of any socially and educationally backward classes or for the Scheduled Castes and Tribes." Equal treatment holds only when there is reasonable basis for differentiation.

Art. 16 : (1) "There shall be equality of opportunity for all citizens in matters relating to employment or any appointment to any office under the State". This does not prevent the State from making provision for reservation in favour of backward classes (3 and 4).

Art. 17 : "Untouchability is abolished and its practice in any form is forbidden. The enforcement of any disability arising out of 'untouchability' shall be an offence punishable in accordance with law."

2. Right to Freedom

Artical 19 of the Constitution guarantees six fundamental freedoms.

Art.19 : (1) All citizens shall have the right —

(a) "to freedom of speech and expression". Reasonable restrictions may be made in its exercise "in the interests of the sovereignty and integrity of India, the security of the State, friendly relations with foreign States, decency and morality, or in relation to contempt of court, defamation or incitement of any offence."

(b) "to assemble peacefully and without arms". Reasonable restrictions may be enacted "in the interests of the sovereignty and integrity of India, or public order or morality." This includes the right to hold meetings, and to take out processions.

(c) "to form associations or unions" with the same restrictions.

(d) and (e) "to move freely" and "to reside and settle" in any part of the territory of India. Reasonable restrictions may be placed "either in the interests of the general public or for the protection of the interests of any Scheduled Tribe."

(f) The 44th Amendment, 1978, has deleted the right to property from this list and made it a statutory right under Part XII, Finance, Property, Contracts and Suits. Art. 300A: "No person shall be deprived of his property save by authority of law."

(g) "to practise any profession or to carry on any occupation, trade or business". Reasonable restrictions may be enacted. "In the interests of the general public" or requiring the necessary technical or professional qualities, or because of State monopolies, directly or through corporations.

Art. 20 : (1) "No one shall be convicted of any offence except for violation of law in force at the time of the commission of the act charged as an offence", or be subjected to a penalty greater than that which was "in force at the time of the commission of the offence."

(2) "No person shall be prosecuted and punished for the same offence more than once."

(3) "No person accused of any offence shall be compelled to be a witness against himself."

Art. 21 : "No person shall be deprived of his life or personal liberty according to procedure established by law."

The confinement of an undertrial prisoner should be reasonable. The arrest and detention of the person by the police should be strictly under the Code of Criminal Procedure. This right is expressed in the Constitution thus:

Art. 22 : (1) "No person who is arrested shall be detained in custody without being informed, as soon as may be, of the grounds for such arrest nor shall he be denied the right to consult, and to be defended by, a legal practitioner of his choice.

(2) "Every person who is arrested and detained in custody shall be produced before the nearest magistrate within the period of twenty-four hours of such arrest ....

(4) to (7) provide safeguards to those who are arrested under any law for preventive detention.

3. Right Against Exploitation

Art. 23 : (1) "Traffic in human beings and beggar and similar forms of forced labour are punishable in accordance with law."

(2) In imposing compulsory service for public purpose, there shall be no discrimination.

Art. 24 : "No child below the age of fourteen years shall be employed to work in any factory or mine or engaged in any hazardous employment."

4. *Right to Freedom of Religion*

Art. 25 : (1) "Subject to public order, morality, and health,— all persons are equally entitled to freedom of conscience and the right freely to profess, practise and propagate religion." The Supreme Court in January 1979 upheld the Madhya Pradesh Act which made it a penal offence to convert or attempt to convert a person by means of "force, fraud or allurement." A similar Act of Orissa was also upheld.

(2) (a) Economic, financial, political or other activities which may be associated with religious practice can be regulated.

Art. 26 : "Subject to public order, morality and health, every denomination or any section thereof shall have the right —

(a) to establish and maintain institutions for religious and charitable purposes;

(b) to manage its own affairs in matters of religion;

(c) to own and acquire movable and immovable property; and

(d) to administer such property in accordance with the law."

Art. 28 : (1) "No religious instruction shall be provided in any educational institution wholly maintained out of State funds."

(3) When an institution is recognised by the State or receives State funds, no one "shall be required to take part, in religious instruction that may be imparted in such institution or to attend any religious worship that may be conducted in such institution", unless such a person or his guardian has given his consent.

5. Cultural and Educational Right

Art. 29 : (1) Any section of citizens "having a distinct language, script or culture of its own shall have the right to continue the same."

(2) "No citizen shall be denied admission into any educational institution maintained by the State or receiving aid out of State funds on grounds only of religion, race, caste, language, or any of them."

Art. 30 : (1) "All minorities, whether based on religion or language, shall have the right to establish and administer educational institutions of their choice."

(1A) The 44th Amendment Act, deleting property from the list of Fundamental Rights has provided that the "amount fixed for acquisition of minority educational institutions would not restrict or abrogate the right guaranteed under the clause." In practice, this would mean "full" compensation.

(2) The State in granting aid to educational institutions shall not discriminate against minority institutions.

Directive Principles and Fundamental Duties

While Part III of the Constitution deals with individual or political richest, Part IV is concerned with socio-economic rights. These are called Directive Principles of State Policy and are not justifiable. Still, being principles of State policy, at the risk of some semantic confusion, they are called "fundamental in the governance of the country" (Art. 37).

Art. 31 : (1) "The State shall try to promote the welfare of the people by securing and protecting effectively as it may be a social order in which justice, social and political, shall inform all the institutions of national life."

(2) The state shall, in particular, strive to minimise the inequalities, income and endeavour to eliminate inequalities

in status, facilities and opportunities, not only amongst individuals, but also amongst groups of people in different areas or engaged in different vocations.

Fundamental Duties

The 42nd Amendment Act, 1976, added Part IV-A to the Constitution spelling out the Fundamental Duties of every citizen. Without social responsibility on the part of all, human rights detailed in the Constitution could not be effectively safeguarded.

Art. 51-A : "It shall be the duty of every citizen of India:

(a) to abide by the Constitution and respect the ideals and institutions, the National Flag and the National Anthem;

(b) to cherish and follow the noble ideals which inspired our national struggle for freedom;

(c) to uphold and protect the sovereignty, unity and integrity of India;

(d) to defend the country and render national service when called upon to do so;

(e) to promote harmony and the spirit of common brotherhood amongst all the people of India transcending religious, linguistic and regional or sectional diversities; to renounce practices derogatory to women;

(f) to value and preserve the rich heritage of our composite culture;

(g) to protect and improve the natural environment including forests, lakes, rivers and wild life, and to have compassion for living creatures;

(h) to develop the scientific temper; humanism and the spirit of inquiry and reform;

(i) to safeguard public property and to abjure violence;

(j) to strive towards excellence in all spheres of individual and collective activities so that the nation constantly rises to higher levels of endeavour and achievement."

Particular Directive Principles

Art. 39 : "The State shall, in particular, direct its policies towards securing

(a) that the citizens, men, women, equally have the right to adequate means of livelihood;
(b) that the ownership and control of the material resources of the community are so distributed as best to subserve the common good;
(c) that the operation of the economic system does not result in concentration of wealth and means of production to the common detriment;
(d) that there is equal pay for equal work for both men and women;
(e) that the health and strength of worker, men and women, and the tender age of children are not abused and that citizens are not forced by economic necessity to enter vocations unsuited to their age and strength;
(f) that children are given opportunities and facilities to develop in a healthy manner and in conditions of freedom and dignity and that childhood and youth are protected against exploitation and against moral and material abandonment."

Art. 39-A : "The State shall secure that the operation of the legal system promotes justice, on a basis of equal opportunity, and shall, in particular, provide for free legal aid, by suitable legislation or schemes or in any other way, to ensure that the opportunities for securing justice are not denied to any citizen by reason of economic or other disabilities."

Art. 40 : "The State shall take steps to organize village panchayats and endow them with such powers and authority as may be necessary to enable them to function as units of self-government."

Art. 41 : "The State shall, within the limits of its economic power capacity, make effective provision for securing the right to work, to education and to public assistance in cases of unemployment, old age, sickness, and disablement, and in other cases of undeserved want."

Art. 42 : "The State shall make provision for just and humane conditions of work and fair maternity relief."

Art. 43 : "The State shall endeavour to secure, by suitable legislation or economic organization or in any other way, to all workers, agricultural or otherwise, work, a living wage, conditions of work ensuring a decent standard of life and for enjoyment of leisure and social and cultural opportunities and, in particular, the State shall endeavour to promote cottage industries on an individual or co-operative basis in rural areas."

Art. 43A : Records the provision of the 42nd Amendment Act, 1976, asking the State "to secure the participation of workers in the management of undertakings, establishments or other organizations engaged in industry."

Art. 44 : "The State shall endeavour to secure for the citizens a uniform civil code throughout the territory of India."

Art. 45 : "The State shall endeavour to promote within a period of ten years.......for free and compulsory education for, all children until they complete the age of fourteen years."

Art. 46 : "The State shall promote with special care the educational and economic interest of the weaker sections of the people, and in particular of the Scheduled Castes and Scheduled Tribes, and shall protect them from all social injustice and all forms of exploitation."

Art. 47 : "The State shall regard the raising the level of nutrition and the standard of public health as among its primary duties and, in particular..... to bring about prohibition of the consumption except for medicinal purpose of intoxicating drinks and drugs which are injurious to health." It urges to improve people's standard of living and public health.

Art. 48 : "The State shall endeavour to organize agriculture, and animal husbandry on modern and scientific lines."

Art. 48-A : Records the provision of the 42nd Amendment Act, 1976, asking the State "to endeavour to protect and improve the environment and to safeguard the forests and the wild life of the country." Again, the amended Constitution shows concern for ecological rights of human persons. It prevents the pollution of water.

Art. 49 : "It shall be the obligation of the State to protect every monument or place or object of artistic or historic interest to be of national importance from spoilation, disfigurement, removal, disposal or export as the case may be."

Art. 50 : "The State shall take steps to separate the judiciary from the executive in the public service of the State."

Art. 51 : Asks the State to promote international peace and harmony.

The Indian Constitution is quite strong on human rights. It asserts the freedom of individuals to live with dignity, but the fundamentalist forces are challenging today the secular nature of our country. (Refer, J.N. Pandey, *Constitutional Law of India,* p.70ff; George V. Lobo, *Human Rights in Indian Situation*, pp.55-65).

9

LEGAL PERSPECTIVES ON HUMAN RIGHTS

The legal directives on human rights are found on different issues related to women, tribals, dalits, ecology, minorities and freedom of religion. The reflections here are mostly based on Indian legal system.

Women's Rights

Indian Constitution ensures the equality of men and women. The exploitation of women is curtailed. The constitutional provisions protect the dignity of women.

Art. 14 : of the Constitution insists that the State will not send up any person equality before the law. Equal protection of law is guaranteed. No discrimination on the basis of sex is permitted.

Art.15 : of the Constitution insists that the State shall not discriminate against any citizen on grounds of religion, race, caste, sex or place of birth. Article 16(1) and 16(2) prohibits discrimination in general, and also discrimination because of sex in offices and those employed under the State. Gender discrimination is not permitted.

Art. 39(a) : of the Constitution asserts that the State shall in particular, direct its policy towards securing that citizens, men and women equally, have the right to an adequate mean of livelihood.

Art. 39(b) : of the Constitution ensures equal pay for equal work. There is clear discrimination found in some sectors in this regard as men are usually paid more than women though the amount of labour force is same.

Art. 39(c) : of the Constitution requires that the State secures health and strength of workers, men and women and that children are not abused and citizens are not forced by economic necessity to enter avocations unsuited to their age and strength.

Art. 51A(c) : of the Constitution insists that it is the duty of every citizen of India to renounce practices derogatory to the dignity of women. (P.D. Mathew and P.M. Bakshi, *Women and the Constitution*, p.1ff).

Though Constitution provides rights for women, most of the Indian women are not aware of their rights. According to M.J. Antony, "While women in the west had to fight for over a century to get some of their basic rights, like right to vote, the Constitution of India gave women right with men from the beginning" (*Women's Rights*, p.1).

The Factories Act, 1948 protects the women at the workplace. It directs to improve the working conditions. Section 27 bans employment of women and children in cotton pressing. If they are employed, specific measures should be taken to safeguard them. Section 48 urges to establish creches if the factory employs 30 or more women. They are to take care of children of women workers. No women can be insisted to work more than nine hours a day (section 66). No women shall also be required to work except between 6a.m. and 7p.m. (*Women's Rights,* p.15 ff).

Dowry System is an evil which prevails in the society. Men demand dowry and it becomes a way to make woman a commodity or object. The right and dignity of women are curtailed. In 1961 Dowry Prohibition Act was passed to prohibit the practice of giving and taking dowry. It is noted that Dowry Act was amended in 1984 to make the practice of dowry a cognizable offence. Dowry is property or valuable security given by one party to a marriage to the other party in connection with the marriage. It is permitted that the gifts can be given freely and voluntarily in proportion to the financial capacity of the giver. Demanding dowry can cause imprisonment for a minimum of six months or a maximum of two years and a fine up to Rs. 10,000 (P.D. Mathew, *The Dowry Prohibition Act, 1961*, p.1ff).

Rape is a human right violation and it challenges the dignity of women. It is done as women are considered as an object. Section 375 of the Indian Penal Code defines rape as it is committed when a man has sexual intercourse with a woman : (1) against her will or (2) without her consent, or (3) with her consent, when her consent has been obtained by putting her or any person in whom is interested, in fear of death, or of hurt, or (4) with her consent, when he by deception, make her believe that he is her lawful husband or (5) with her consent, given on account of her unsoundness of mind, or intoxication, when she is incapable of understanding the consequence of her consent or (6) with or without her consent, when she is under 16 years of age. The rape is a severe offence and hence a police officer can arrest the accused without warrant. Normal punishment for rape is minimum 7 to 10 years of imprisonment and maximum life imprisonment and fine. (P.D. Mathew, *The Law on Rape*, pp.2-13).

Kidnapping and abduction are violation of women's rights. Kidnapping means stealing a child, a boy under 18 years and a girl under 16 years or any person of unsound mind. It refers to minors. Abduction refers to adult women taken away by force or deceit. According to M.J. Antony "Kidnapping or abducting a women to compel her to marry any person against her will, or to force or induce her to illicit intercourse will be punishable with 10 years imprisonment." (*Women's Rights*, p.97). The child molestation and sexual act with minors are also severe offences. Insulting the women is also considered as a serious crime. Section 509 of Indian Penal Code defines the insult to women as uttering any word, making any sound or gesture or exhibits any object, intending that such word or sound shall be heard or that such gesture or object shall be seen by such women or intrudes upon the privacy of such woman. It is a punishable crime.

The Commercial Sex Workers (CSW) are arguing for their rights, though the traditional outlook towards them is not welcoming. Prostitution is an evil. But one has to look to the context in which it is developed. The society is largely contributing to this institution. The poverty is one of the problems that is related to prostitution so also other economic issues. The Suppression of Immoral Traffic in Women and Girls Act, 1956 (SITA) was amended in 1986 as Central Government introduced the Immoral Traffic in Persons Prevention Act.

Jean D'Cunha defines patriarchy as man's control over woman's sexuality, fertility/reproduction and labour power. For her the institution of prostitution is the other side of male domination and class oppression of woman (*The Legalization of Prostitution*, p.15-16). SITA (1956) aims at abolishing traffic in women and girls for prostitution. So it penalizes brothel keeping, pimping, procuring, detention of a woman or girl for prostitution and seduction of a woman in custody. The practice of prostitution individually, independently and voluntarily by a woman does not constitute an offence. But punishment was given when there is prostitution in or near a public place and seduction and soliciting for prostitution (*Ibid.*, p.43). Interestingly, SITA criminalize the prostitute and set free the client which is an example for double morality and challenging the woman's rights. D'Cunha observes that penalties imposed on prostitutes are far more severe than those on brothel-keepers and pimps.

The severe human right violation is that even children are kidnapped and sold to the brothel-keepers as it is a lucrative trade. It is observed by D'Cunha that a minor girl who is a virgin is sold for anything between Rs. 500 and Rs. 7000 in Kamatiputra. Immoral Traffic in Persons Prevention Act, 1986 (ITTPA) includes both male and female (not merely females) who engage in prostitution. It also defines prostitution as any form of sexual exploitation or abuse or commercial purpose. There is also organizations of prostitutes for their rights. They demand the legalization and licensing of prostitutes. They protest the police harassment. Their organizations include 'the Bharatiya Patita Udhar Sabha', 'The Aashaya Tirskrut Nari Sangh' and 'The Pune Devadasi Sangatna'. The International Committee for Prostitute's Right has drawn up a world charter for their rights which guarantees the prostitutes all human rights and liberties including the freedom of speech, travel, immigration, work, marriage and motherhood and the right to unemployment insurance, health insurance and housing (*Ibid.*, pp.110-112,144).

The prostitution is an evil which is necessitated in the society because of sociological and economic factors. Prostitutes are the marginalized group who are to be rehabilitated, as a structure should be created to reinstate them. The society contributes to prostitution as it is irresponsible and it is male chauvinistic. Crisis is found in dealing with their issue. It is important to protect the rights as a prostitute, at the same time, redeeming the prostitutes from this evil situation is another responsibility.

Indian Marriage Laws and Human Rights

The Indian Constitution affirms the secularism and equality. The different religions and their ideals co-exist in this country. The family laws are important in Indian context, every religious tradition has their own personal laws. The family law includes marriage, sonship, maintenance, devolution of property and even charity endowments. In the religiously and ethically pluralistic country like India, the British recognized the personal laws. (Rajkumar, Agarwala, "Preface", *Conversion and Indian Civil Law,* by Julian Saldanha, Banglore: Theological Publications in India, 1981, p.5). The Hindus, Muslims, Christians, Parsis and Jews have their own personal laws. The 'Hindu' comprises of Hinduism, Buddhism, Jainism and Sikhism in the personal law (Paras Diwan and Peeyushi Diwan, *Family Law,* (2nd edn.), Allahabad: Allahabad Law Agency, 1994, p.4). The persons who is a convert or re-convert to Jainism, Buddhism, Sikhism or Hinduism is also a Hindu according to law. This section deals with the Hindu, Muslim, Christian and Parsi personal laws which deals with sexuality and marriage.

The Hindu Personal Law

The Hindu Marriage Act was enacted by the parliament on 18th May, 1955 (Act No. XXV of 1955). This Act applies to:

(a) any person who is a Hindu by religion in any of its forms or developments, including a Virashaiva, a Lingayat or a follower of the Brahma, Prarthana or Arya Samaj;
(b) any person who is a Buddhist, Jain or Sikh by religion;
(c) any other person domiciled in the territories to which this Act extends, who is not a Muslim, Christian, Parsi

or Jew by religion. The following persons are Hindus, Buddhists, Jainists or Sikhs by religion :

(i) any child, legitimate or illegitimate, both of whose parents are Hindus, Buddhists, Jainists or Sikhs by religion.
(ii) any child, legitimate or illegitimate, one of whose parents is a Hindu, Buddhist, Jaina or Sikh by religion and who is brought up as a member of the tribe, community, group or family to which such parents belong.
(iii) any person who is a convert or re-convert to the Hindu, Buddhist, Jaina or Sikh religion (Central Law Agency, *The Hindu Law Acts*, Allahabad: Central Law Agency, 1995, p.3, cf., Asutosh Mookerjee, *Marriage Separation and Divorce,* Calcutta: S.C. Sankar and Sona Ltd., 1986, p.263).

The Conditions for Hindu marriage follow :

(i) neither party has a spouse living at the time of marriage;
(ii) at the time of marriage, neither party —

(a) is incapable of giving valid consent to it in consequence of unsoundness of mind; or
(b) though capable of giving a valid consent, has been suffering from mental disorder of such a kind or such an extent as to be unfit for marriage and the procreation of children; or
(c) has been subject to recurrent attacks of insanity or epilepsy;

(iii) the bridegroom has completed the age of twenty-one years and the bride the age of eighteen years at the time of marriage;

(iv) the parties are not within the degrees of prohibited relationship unless the custom or usage governing each of them permits a marriage between the two;

(v) the parties are not *sapindars* (a relationship with reference to any person extends as far as the third generation in the line of ascent through the mother, and the fifth in the line of ascent through the father. In each cause the person concerned is counted as the first generation) of each other, unless the custom or usage governing each of them permits of a marriage between the two. (Asutosh Mookerjee, *Marriage Separation and Divorce,* Calcutta: S.C. Sarkar and Sons Ltd., 1986, p.270).

According to the Hindu Marriage Act (1955), no Hindu male can have more than one wife and no Hindu female can have more than one husband. The Hindu widows can remarry. According to this Act, no Hindu can marry a non-Hindu. But they can enter into what is known as "civil marriage" through the Special Marriage Act, 1954. The inter-caste marriages are permitted. The marriage between near relations like cousins or uncles and nieces allowed only if their customs allow such marriage (P.D. Mathew, P.M. Bakshi, *Hindu Marriage and Divorce,* New Delhi : Indian Social Institute, 1994, pp. 2-3).

The impotency, the unsound mind (insanity), the discovery that the wife is pregnant at the time of marriage, the consent of the person is obtained by force, the spouse is not willing to cohabit with the party are the clauses by which annulment of marriage is possible (*Ibid.,* p.73, Paras Diwan and Peeyushi Diwan, *Family Law, op.cit.*, p.90.). The grounds for divorce are : (1) adultery (it means a voluntary sexual intercourse between persons not married), (2) treating with cruelty, (3) desertion for at least two years (Desertion is conduct by way of permanent forsaking of marital obligations), (4) conversion to another religion, (5) incurable insanity of mental order, (6) incurable and virulent leprosy, (7) venereal disease in a communicable form, (8) renouncing the world and becoming a *sanyasi*, (9) not being heard of for seven years, (10) non-resumption of cohabitation after a decree of judicial separation, for at least one year, (11) non-compliance with a decree of restitution of conjugal rights for at least one year, (12) husband being guilty of rape or unnatural sex after marriage, (13) husband failing to pay the wife maintenance ordered by court (P.D. Mathew, P.M. Bakshi, *Hindu Marriage and Divorce,* Indian Social Institute, New Delhi, 1994, p.8; Asutosh Mookerjee, *Marriage, Separation and Divorce, op.cit.,* pp.283-291) and (14) by mutual consent. According to Asutosh Mookerjee the bigamy is also a ground for divorce according to the Hindu Marriage Act (Asutosh Mookerjee, *Marriage, Separation and Divorce, op.cit.,* p.289).

The remarriage is possible after the period of appeal against the decree has expired (*The Hindu Law Acts, op.cit.,* p.12). The Hindu Marriage Law is very much concerned of the sanctity of marriage. The conjugality is given importance that it advises to cohabit with spouse and the impotency and ill-health are taken seriously to become the causes for divorce. The illicit sex and the bestiality are seriously dealt with. The question is whether insanity and ill-health after marriage can be a ground for divorce.

The Muslim Personal Law

The Muslim Personal Law is one of the most controversial laws in India. The Muslim Personal Law (Shariat) Act, 1937 is applicable to all Mohammedans. A Mohammedan is anyone who acknowledges that there is only one God and Mohammed is the prophet. (Asutosh Mookerjee, *Marriage, Separation and Divorce, op.cit.*, p.24). The Sunnis and Shias are the major sects in Islam. The Khojas and Cutihi Memons of Bombay are originally Hindus, but are subjected to Shariah Law and they are converted to Islam. A Mohammedan male can marry a *Kitabia* (a female believer in Christianity or Judaism). This marriage is a valid one. But a Mohammedan women cannot contract a valid marriage with a male believer in Christianity or Judaism. However, the Muslim woman's marriage with a non-Muslim is merely irregular and not void (*Ibid.*, p.25). Under Shia Law the marriage between a Muslim and non-Muslim is unlawful and void. But the Muslim male may contract a valid *Muta* (temporary marriage for enjoyment) marriages with some non-Muslims (*Ibid.*, p.25). The Muslim belongs to different sects can marry each other. So the inter- sect marriages are allowed.

The observations and analysis of P.D. Mathew and P.K. Bakshi go like this : The Muslim male can have four wives. But the Muslim female cannot have more than one husband. The Muslim (male or female) who has attained puberty and is of sound mind can marry (Child marriage is prohibited under the Child Marriage Restraint Act, 1929. But it does not nullify the marriage, though it leads to punishment). If a Muslim has not attained puberty, he or she can be married by his or her guardian (P.D. Mathew and P.K. Bhakshi, *Muslim Marriage and Divorce,* New Delhi: Indian Social Institute, New Delhi 1989, pp.6-7.)

The prohibited degree of relationship (marriage) are as follows: One cannot marry,

1. One's own mother or grandmother
2. One's daughter or granddaughter
3. One's sister (full or consanguine)
4. One's own niece or grand niece

5. One's own aunt or great aunt (paternal / maternal)
6. The ascendants and descendants of one's wife
7. The wife of one's ascendant or descendant. (*Ibid.*, pp.8-9.)

The Divorce is of Various Categories

(a) Extra judicial divorce, divorce at the instance of the husband unilaterally and without requiring any ground (This is the populous 'Talaq' formula).

(b) Extra judicial divorce at the initiative of the husband under constructive category. It is called a 'constructive' category. It is divorce in the form of Ila and Zihar at the initiative of the husband. The husband takes a vow of abstinence from sexual intercourse for at least four months and when the vow is fulfilled, it means divorce. This is the Ila form of divorce which would be settled by the judiciary. In Zihar form the husband compares his wife within the prohibited degrees for marriage (Such as comparing the wife to the mother). On the husband making such announcement the wife become entitled to seek judicial divorce.

(c) Extra judicial divorce by mutual consent as confirmed by statute.

(d) Judicial divorce at the instance of the wife, on specified grounds in statute (*Ibid.*, pp.11, 14-15).

The *Talaq* is a very complex issue today in India. Even in the absence of wife, the *Talaq* can be pronounced. It is a unilateral divorce by the husbands. According to Shia Law, it must be pronounced orally before two competent witnesses. The Sunni Law prescribes that Talaq may be pronounced orally or in writing. The *Talaq* may be pronounced as it is said below :

(a) A single pronouncement during the woman's Tuhr (period between two menstruations). This must be followed abstinence during *iddat*. It becomes effective and irrevocable when *iddat* expires (Ahsan).

(b) Three pronouncements made during three successive tuhrs. There should be abstinence during all the three tuhrs. Divorce is complete and irrevocable on the third pronouncement (Hasan).

(c) A triple pronouncement made during the tuhr in one sentence (I divorce thee thrice) or three separate pronouncements during one tuhr such as "I divorce thee. I divorce thee. I divorce thee" (Talak-ul-bidaat).

(d) One pronouncement (single) during tuhr indicating an intention to divorce irrevocably. It is effective and irrevocable, the moment it is pronounced (Talak-ul-bidaat). A Muslim wife cannot use Talaq in order to divorce her husband (*Ibid.*, pp.12-13, cf. Asutosh Mookerjee, *Marriage, Separation and Divorce, op.cit.*, pp.80-83.).

The Muslim wife can sue for divorce under the Act of 1939 on the following reasons :

(a) The whereabouts of the husband is/are not known for a period of four years.

(b) Husbands failure or neglect to provide maintenance to the wife.

(c) Husband being sentenced to imprisonment for a period of seven years or more.

(d) Husband's failure without reasonable cause to perform marital obligation for a period of three years or more.

(e) Husband being impotent at the time of marriage and continuing to be so till filing of the suit.

(f) Husband's insanity for at least two years or husband's suffering from leprosy or virulent venereal disease.

(g) Exercise of right of "repudiation" of marriage by the wife (A wife married by her guardians while she is below the age of 15 years, can repudiate the marriage before attaining age of 18 years provided the marriage has not been consummated).

(h) Husband's cruelty (husband's association with woman of evil repute, husband's attempt to force the wife to lead an immoral life, husband's obstructing the wife in the observance of her religion practices, husband's unequal treatment of one of his wives, where he has more than one wife) (*Ibid.*, pp.17-19).

There was also a question whether a Muslim woman could get maintenance after divorce. In the famous Mohammed Ahmed Khan *Vs*. Shah Bano (985), the Supreme Court held that the husband must continue to maintain her until her remarriage. But this has undergone change under the law passed by the parliament. The new legislation says that after idaat the wife can get maintenance from the relatives who are her potential heirs. The husband's liability ceases with the idaat (three menstrual courses after the date of divorce — this means three months). Failing maintenance by above relatives, the wife can get maintenance from the Wakf Board (*Ibid.*, pp.19-20).

The remarriage is allowed to Muslim women with certain conditions. "Under Muslim Law, after dissolution of marriage, by divorce or death a woman is required to wait for certain period, before the expiry of which she cannot remarry." (Paras Diwan, Peeyushi Diwan, *Family Law, op.cit.*, p.184). In the case of the dissolution of consummated marriage by divorce, the wife is required to perform idda of three months. If she is pregnant the idda will continue till she delivers the child. The Muslim law insists that the husband too cannot remarry during the period wife is undergoing idda. When the marriage is dissolved by death, the wife is to observe the idda of four lunar months and ten days (*Ibid.*, p.184. *Ibid.*, p.184).

Most of the conservative Muslim scholars are not willing to modify the Shariat or Muslim personal law in believing that the author of Shariah is God himself (Muitahid-al-Asr Maulana Syed Ali Naqi, "Can the Shariah-Laws be modified?" *Muslim Law,* edited by F.R. Faridi and M.N. Siddiqui, Aligarh: Islamic-Research Circle, 1973, p.12). Maulana Mohammed Ishaq Sandelvi feels that "Muslim Personal Law, is in fact, another name of the cultural and social freedom of the Indian Muslims." (Moulana Mohammed Ishaq Sandelvi "Muslim Personal Law", *Muslim Personal Law* edited by F.R. Faridi and M.N. Siddiqui, *op.cit.*, p.16). The Muslims have a close affinity towards their personal law, and they do not favour the modification or reform of it. They also reject the idea of a uniform civil code. For Ishaq Sandelvi, the Shariat is a set of eternal and times rules. Arun Shourie the journalist and social scientist argues for the reform in the Muslim Personal Law in the wake of Shah Bano controversy. But the Muslim fundamentalists are totally for protecting the existing Shariah. [Arun Shourie, "The Shariat", *The Illustrated Weekly of India* (January 5, 1986), p.7]. Shourie argues to re-examine the Muslim personal law in the light of modern secular principles, since he feels that what is known as Shariah today is more the creation of clerics and magistrates than of the Quran and the practice of the prophet.

The Talaq controversy is also a watershed in the Indian situation. A decree issued by Jamat-e-Ahle Hadis states that the pronouncement of talaq in a row is invalid. According to Sheik Ataur Madani, "A month has to pass before the husband can pronounce a talaq for a second time and another month for it to be pronounced a third time." [Ranjit Bhushan, "A Separate Identity", *Indian Express* (Sunday Magazine), (July 11, 1993) p.3]. Furqan Ahmed also criticises the ignorance of Indian men who used triple talaq in a row which is against the original intention of Shariah. The triple talaq is also sometimes approved by the Maulavis and judicial court to make divorce irrevocable. These are mistakes. According to Furqan Ahmed, "Under the law of divorce derived from the Quranic injunctions and teachings of the prophet, 'triple talaq' can never be accepted as a weapon against women with all its injustice." ["Understanding Islamic Divorce", *Indian Express* (August 1, 1993), p.8]. In the words of Seema Alavi, the Talaq is a unilateral act. Since the Islam condemns divorce, so the simplistic means of divorce is inhuman and suicidal. ["Talaq, Talaq, Talaq". *In Indian Express* (February 27, 1994), p.10]. Shenaaz Sheikh was looking for companionship and equality from her husband, but he made her home a prison. When she demanded her rights, triple talaq was the result. [Shenaaz Sheikh, "A Muslim Woman Speaks Out", *Indian Express* (December 9, 1994), p.8].

The present Muslim Personal Law badly affects the women. The proper perspective is lacking when Shariah is exercised. However, the Orthodox Muslims and scholars are rigid and not for attempting a humane interpretation of it. The Shariah which is found in the enactment of 1937 protects the importance of sexuality as the husbands cannot move as they like. They are insisted to cohabit, and if not after two years it can lead to divorce. The impotence is also given as a reason to divorce, since the conjugal right of women cannot be entertained by an impotent man. The marriage is not seriously understood by Muslims as the divorce is quite easy for men even for simple reason. It can lead to irresponsible marriage relationship.

The Parsi Personal Law

The Parsi Marriage and Divorce Act was enacted in 1936. (Act III of 1936). The Act applies to Parsi Zoroastrians of India. The consanguinity or affinity can be a cause for making a Parsi marriage unlawful. Bigamy is not allowed. Remarriage is not permitted unless there is a proper dissolution of the first contract (Asutosh Mookerjee, *Marriage, Separation and Divorce, op.cit.*, p.359).

The grounds for divorce are following :

(a) that the marriage has not been consummated within one year after its solemnization owing to the wilful refusal of the spouse;
(b) the unsound mind;
(c) pre-marital pregnancy;
(d) that the spouse committed adultery or bigamy or rape;
(e) that the husband has compelled the wife to submit her to prostitution;
(f) that the spouse is imprisoned for seven years;
(g) that the husband or wife deserts the partner for at least three years;
(h) that the decree or the order for judicial separation has been passed against the defendant, or an order has been passed against the defendant by a Magistrate awarding separate maintenance to the plaintiff and the parties have not had marital intercourse for three years or more since such decree or order;
(i) that the defendant has failed to comply with a decree for restitution of conjugal rights for a year or more;

(j) that the husband or wife ceases to be a Parsi by converting to another religion (*Ibid.*, p.366).

The Parsi personal law seriously deals with the irresponsibility in marriage. The conjugal rights are given extreme importance by the law. The married partners are to lead a responsible life. They are not to be involved in adultery or bigamy. The living together is also encouraged by the law.

The Christian Personal Law

The Indian Christian Marriage Act (Act XV of 1872) is the main point of discussion in this section. The term 'Indian Christian' includes the Christian descendants of native of India converted to Christianity. The expression Christian means persons professing the Christian religion. The valid marriage should be solemnized if one or both persons is or are a Christian or Christians (*The Indian Christian Marriage Act,* Allahabad: Allahabad Law Agency, n.d., p.6).

The law relating to divorce among Christians in India can be found in the Indian Divorce Act, 1869. The Christian husband can seek divorce on the ground that his wife is guilty of adultery. The wife can seek divorce by the following grounds:

(a) Husband's conversion to another religion and his having gone through a form of marriage with another woman;
(b) Husband's being guilty of incestuous adultery (Adultery is sexual relations by a married person with a person to whom he or she is not married : Incestuous adultery is defined in Section 2(6) of Indian Divorce Act on adultery committed by a husband with a woman with whom, if his wife were dead, he could not lawfully contract marriage by reason of her being within the

prohibited degrees of consanguinity or affinity);

(c) Husband's bigamy, coupled with adultery;

(d) Husband's marriage with another woman coupled with adultery;

(e) Husband's being guilty of rape, sodomy or bestiality;

(f) Husband's adultery coupled with cruelty;

(g) Husband's adultery, coupled with desertion without reasonable excuse, for two years or upwards (desertion implies an abandonment against the wish of the person changing it. (P.D. Mathew and P.M. Bakshi, *Christian Law of Divorce,* 3rd Reprint, New Delhi: Indian Social Institute, 1993, p.5).

The marriage can be nullified under the Indian Divorce Act on the following reasons:

(a) Respondent (opposite party) was impotent at the time of marriage and at the time of institution of the suit;

(b) Parties are within prohibited degree of relationship;

(c) Either party was a lunatic or idiot at the time of marriage; or

(d) The former spouse of either party was living at the time of marriage and the marriage was then in force (*Ibid.*, p.11; Paras Diwan and Peeyushi Diwan, *Family Law, op.cit.*, p.89).

The Christian divorce law is said to be unfair to women. The women cannot seek divorce for mere adultery of her husband. But the husband can divorce his wife just for adultery. The conditional adultery is saving the husband. It is conditional since the adultery should be coupled with incest, cruelty, sexual perversion, bigamy or desertion in the case of husband.

According to P.M. Bakshi, the same criteria (adultery as a cause for divorce unconditionally) should be applicable for both husband and wife. He states, "One would have expected that the same remedy would be available to the wife. But unfortunately this is not so [P.M. Bakshi, "Christian Divorce Law unfair to woman", *Indian Express* (March 27, 1984), p.8]. There is a move from the progressive men and women to seek a revision of the Indian Christian Marriage Act and law of divorce. Updating the laws are always important. Annie Thayil, the lawyer also pointed out that, the Christian law of divorce is unfair to women. ["Christian Marriage Law", *Religion and Society,* Vol. XXXI, No. 1 (March, 1984), p.15].

The Special Marriage Act

The Special Marriage Act was enacted in 1954. This Act is found as an improvement upon the old Act of 1872 which it repeals and contains additions deemed necessary to enable the society to keep pace with the march of civilization in modern times is that it permits inter-communal and inter-caste marriages *(The Special Marriage Act, 1954*, Allahabad: Central Law Agency, 1955, p.5). It is enacted as Act No. 43 of 1954.

The conditions for marriage under the special marriage is as follows:

The prohibited relationship includes:

1. Relationship by half or uterine blood as well as by full blood ('full blood' and 'half blood'—two persons are said to be related to each other by full blood when they are descended from a common ancestor by the same wife and by half blood when they are descended from a common ancestor but by different wives);

2. Illegitimate blood relationship as well as legitimate;
3. Relationship by adoption as well as by blood.

The following conditions are to be met by the husband and wife for the solemnization of marriage :

1. Neither party has a spouse living;
2. Neither party is incapable of giving a valid consent in consequence of unsoundness of mind;
3. Neither party is suffering from epilepsy or insanity or impotency;
4. The parties are not within the degree of prohibited relationship;
5. The male has completed the age of 21 and the female 18 years (*Ibid.*, pp.2-3).

The marriage can be nullified if :— (a) the marriage has not been consummated owing to the wilful refusal of the respondent to consummate marriage, or (b) the respondent was pregnant at the time of marriage by some other person than the petitioner; or (c) the consent of either party to marriage was obtained by fraud. The divorce can be sought by the husband or wife on the following grounds :

(a) The voluntary sexual intercourse with any person other than his or her spouse,
(b) Desertion of the spouse for a continuous period not less than two years,
(c) Spouse is undergoing a sentence of imprisonment for seven years for an offence as defined in the Indian Penal Code (Act XLV of 1860),
(d) Cruelty,
(e) Incurable mental disorder,

(f) Suffering from venereal disease in a communicable form,

(g) Suffering from leprosy,

(h) Not been heard of as being alive for a period of seven years or more by those persons who would naturally have heard of the spouse if the spouse had been alive. (*Ibid.*, pp.8-9; Asutosh Mookerjee, *Marriage, Separation and Divorce*, *op.cit.*, pp.399-404).

The Special Marriage Act does not allow polyandry or polygyny. A person marries under this Act should not have any other spouse (P.D. Mathew, P.M. Bakshi, *Special Marriage Act*, New Delhi: Indian Socal Institute, 1991, p.3). Though the personal laws on marriage and divorce in the Indian law system is giving ample provisions for divorce, the Christian church or other religious communities will allow divorce by those reasons stated in the Marriage Acts. Most of the Christian Churches in India will not usually permit divorce after the consummation of marriage. The law of each communities differ one another. While monogamy is the principle of Christian personal law, polygyny is permitted by Muslim Personal Law. The personal laws are stressing mostly the normative principles.

The Personal Laws and Uniform Civil Code

Though there is no unanimity over the issue of the common or Uniform Civil Code among the different religious leaders, this idea is in the air. It is a controversial topic. While the Hindu religious leaders advocate for Uniform Civil Code, the Muslims are suspicious of it. Since there is different personal laws which conflict each other, the need for a uniform civil code is being discussed today.

Each religious communities were permitted to follow its personal laws in the field of marriage, divorce, inheritance, succession, gifts and adoption of children by the non-interference policy of British rules [Thomas Kadankavil, "Editorial", *The Journal of Dharma,* Vol. XI, No.3 (July-Sep. 1986), p.215].

Later most of the personal laws are accepted by the enactment of the Indian Government. The question about the uniform civil code came up in the Constituent Assembly of India soon after the independence. According to Fr. Kadankavil, "The main supportive thought behind this thinking was that secularism clearly demands a Uniform Family Law, and that separate family laws for different communities would result in discrimination between the communities which is repugnant to the secular character of the state (*Ibid.*, p.215).

The debate over the issue of the Uniform Civil Code came out with the following clause which was adopted as Article 44 (Article 44 appears as 'Directive Principles of State Policy', Part IV, Articles 36-50) in the Indian Constitution: "The State shall endeavour to secure for the citizens a Uniform Civil Code throughout the territory of India" (*Ibid.*, p.215). The 'Directive principles' were not conceived to be mandatory. According to Fr.Thomas Kadankavil, "If the directive concerning the Uniform Civil Code is made mandatory, it would go against the following fundamental right enunciated in Article 25 : subject to public order, morality and health and to other provisions of this part, all persons are equally entitled to freedom of this part, all persons are equally entitled to freedom of conscience and the right to freely profess, practice and propagate religion" (*Ibid.*, p.216).

Tahir Mohmood is suspicious of those who advocate for Uniform Civil Code. He states, "The slogan of a Uniform Civil Code seems to have been adopted by as a camouflage to attempt wiping off the cultural traditions of all the religious minorities in India [Tahir Mohmood, "Uniform *vs*. Common Civil Code in India", *The Journal of Dharma,* Vol. XI, No. 3 (July-September,1986) p.228]. According to S.N. Balasundaram,

"The desire for a common civil code in India is a thrust towards modernity in traditional society which seeks to weld the mutually exclusive communal and religious groups into a united and viable society. It is a laudable but difficult to attempt at laying the foundations of secularism which is envisaged by our Constitution and, in the context of a religiously pluralistic society means an equal respect to all religions, though thus is not the meaning in which westerners understand the concept [S.N. Balasundaram, "The Conflict Between Tradition and Modernity," *The Journal of Dharma,* Vol. XI, No.3 (July-Septmber 1986), p.230].

Balasundaram sees the positive elements of a Uniform Civil Code as he states, "By fostering the secular democratic values of liberty, equality and fraternity which form the ideological basis of our Constitution, we can build an integrated nation. One of the practical means of strengthening the bond of political unity between the different religious communities is to lay the firm base for an integrated Indian Society. It is in this context that the framing of a common civil code assumes great significance. For such a code reflecting the secular spirit of the Constitution would strengthen the existing social bonds and foster the political integration of the different religious communities by subjecting them to a common judicial procedure in respect of the personal law" (*Ibid.*, pp.237-238).

Though the discussion over the Uniform Civil Code is there, it is difficult to come to the agreement on how to do that in religiously and ethical pluralistic society. The Hindus, the Jainists, Buddhists, Islam, Sikhs, Parsees and Christians have their culture, the values and perspectives on the issues like sexuality and marriage. Unless religious leaders come to certain common understanding it is not easy. Though Tahir Mohmood accepts that the Special Marriage Act of 1954 is understood as a step towards Common Civil Code, there is no one even presented a concrete picture of the form and contents of the proposed code. [S. Tahir Mohmood, "Uniform Civil Code and Islamic Law", *Religion and Society,* Vol. XXVI, No.4 (December, 1979), pp.29, 36].

Asgar Ali Engineer talks about the moulding of Hindu customs so also the Muslim. The reform of the Muslim personal law is desirable in his view. In order to do that we should avoid the terms 'change' or 'reform' but use the phrase 'creative interpretation in the changed context, [Asgar Ali Engineer, "Uniform Civil Code and Indian Muslims", *Religion and Society,* Vol. XXIV, No.4 (December, 1979), p.84].

Asgar Ali Engineer's observation should be noted that it is important to reform the personal laws of different religious communities. This is applicable to Christian personal law also. The prejudice against the women should be avoided from the Christian personal law. It is necessary to make a 'creative interpretation' of the religious texts in the changed context, in order to make the texts and its principles or teachings relevant to the particular community and the community at large.

Instituting certain common norms and principles based on love, justice, equality and humanness is important in any ethically plural context. This can be applied to Indian context also. Asgar Ali Engineer rightly states, "India is a secular nation and as such has to serve all her citizens irrespective of caste or religion on an equal basis and ensuring them all universally accepted human rights. This applies as well to the domain of conjugal relations, inheritance etc. as to any other social or political domain (*Ibid.*, p.80).

Dalits and Human Rights

'*Dalit*' comes from the Sanskrit word '*dal*' which means crushed or oppressed. *Dalits* are the indigenous group in India who constitute the majority of our population who undergo several kinds of violence. Their labour force is exploited as they are given low wages and their dignity is not recognized. They are socially alienated, economically deprived and politically powerless. Their rights and privileges are denied. The *dalit* men and women are the objects of violence of the upper castes. Most of the *dalits* are landless labourers and slaves.

In certain villages the *dalits* are not allowed to draw water from public wells or even to use footwears. Untouchability or pollution challenge the dignity and rights of *dalits* as it dehumanizes them. Caste system itself is a systemic violence as it is a symbol of injustice. It was reported by Felix Wilfred that in 1980 in Kuzhapadi in Tamil Nadu, four *dalit* children were done to death in water by electrocution simply because they dared to take bath in a well belonging to an upper caste man (*Human Right in Indian Situation*, p. vii). Human right violations are happening right in our context but no one is responding to this injustice. It is happening both in the society and church.

The *dalits* are beaten up and burnt to death even by false accusation by the upper caste men. In villages, the dalits become the victims of structure which is controlled by dominant castes. Entry for *dalits* are not permitted in some temples. Some temples are reserved for higher castes, though Indian Constitution upholds dignity and equality of all persons. An incident was reported from North Karnataka in 1987 that caste Hindus forced the *dalits* to eat human excreta. They are also not allowed to participate in the festivals.

It is sad to say that the untouchability is continuing in many parts of the country, though Article 17 of the Indian Constitution has abolished it. Government of India passed the Untouchability (Offences) Acts in 1955 and it was amended in 1976 and known as "Protection of Civil Rights Acts, 1955". Impurity was ascribed to persons belonging to scheduled caste and they were prohibited from entering Hindu temples, public places, streets, public conveyance, eating places and educational institutions. These inhuman practices are banished by the Constitution. No person is permitted to justify the caste system on historical or philosophical grounds. Justifying caste system is punishable.

Constitutional Provisions

(i) Article 15(1) prohibits "the state" from discriminating against any citizen on grounds only of religion, race, caste, sex, place of birth or any of them. This right under Article 15 (i) is available, to the citizens against the State only.

(ii) Article 15(2) prohibits any restriction, disability or liability with regard to, (a) access to shops, public restaurants, hotels and places of public entertainment; or (b) the use of wells, tanks, bathing ghats, roads and places of public resort maintained wholly or partly out of State funds or dedicated to the use of general public, on grounds only of religion, race, caste, etc. This right under Article 15(2) is available to the citizens against any person. However, a private well or tank does not come within the meaning of this clause.

(iii) Similarly Article 16(1) promotes equality of opportunity for all citizens in matters relating to public employment or appointment to any office under the State and Article 16(2) prohibits any discrimination on grounds only of religion, race, caste, etc. in respect of employment or office under the State.

(iv) Similarly Article 17 of the Constitution states, "untouchability is abolished and its practice in any form is forbidden. The enforcement of any disability arising out of untouchability shall be an offence punishable in accordance with law."

(v) Article 23(1) prohibits traffic in human beings and forced labour and thus aims at "recognition and restoration of the dignity of man."

(vi) Article 25(1) guarantees the rights to religion to all persons which includes the right "to freedom of conscience and right freely to profess, practise and propagate religion." But on the ground of religious freedom, no individual can lawfully defend "untouchability".

(vii) Article 25(2) removes the general obstacles which otherwise would have been so in providing for social welfare and reform or the throwing open of Hindu religious institutions of a public character to all classes and sections of Hindus. A Scheduled Caste Hindu has the right to worship in any temple in the same manner and to the same extent as any other non-Scheduled Caste Hindu.

(viii) Article 29(2) states that, "No citizen shall be denied admission into any educational institution maintained by the State or receiving aid out of State funds on grounds only of religion, race, caste, language or any of them."

(ix) Under Article 32, any citizen whose fundamental rights including the right against Untouchability under Article 17 are violated can move the Supreme Court directly by writ proceedings for the enforcement of the rights conferred by the Constitution. Public spirited individuals, lawyers, social workers, journalists and voluntary organisations can on behalf of the Scheduled Castes file Public Interest Litigation petitions in the Supreme Court under Article 32 or in the High Courts under Article 226 of the Constitution.

What are the directive principles of State policy for the development of the Scheduled Castes?

(i) Article 38(1) under Directive Principles of State Policy, provides that, "The State shall strive to promote the welfare of the people by securing and protecting as effectively as it may a social order, in which justice, social, economic and political, shall inform all the institutions of the national life".

(ii) Article 38(2) exhorts the State to eliminate, among other things, inequalities in status, facilities and opportunities.

(iii) Article 39A, which has been added by the Constitution 42nd Amendment Act, 1976, states, "The State shall secure that the operation of the legal system promotes justice. On the basis of equal opportunity, and shall in particular, provide free legal aid, by suitable legislation or schemes or in any other way to ensure that opportunities for securing justice are not denied to any citizen by reason of economic or other disabilities." This provision ought to be a boon to the Scheduled Caste who suffer from economic and social disabilities and as a consequence are deprived of equal opportunities to secure justice.

(iv) Article 46 directs the State to promote with special care the interest of the weaker sections, especially of the Scheduled Castes and Scheduled Tribes, and to protect them from social injustice and exploitation.

What are the other provisions in the Constitution to Safeguard the interests of the Scheduled Castes?

(i) Article 164 provides for the appointment of a minister-in-charge of tribal welfare. He will also be incharge of the welfare of Scheduled Castes and Backward Classes in the State of Bihar, Madhya Pradesh and Orissa.

(ii) Articles 330 and 332 guarantee political justice to the Scheduled Castes who were deliberately deprived of this right previously. These Articles provide for reservation of seats for the Scheduled Castes and Scheduled Tribes in the House of the People and Legislative Assembly of every State.

(iii) Article 338 provides for appointment by the President of a special officer for the Scheduled Castes and Tribes to investigate all matters relating to the safeguards provided for them under the Constitution.

(iv) Article 341 empowers the President to specify castes, races, or tribes to be Scheduled Castes or Scheduled Tribes.

(P.D. Mathew, T. Chacko, *The Law on the Abolition of Untouchability,* pp.3-5).

Dalit Christians and Human Rights

The *dalit* Christians undergo social kinds of oppressions in the Indian context. The unfavourable and unfair attitude of the church and society to the *dalits* is supported by the Indian Constitution. Indian Constitution keeps a prejudice towards the *Dalit* Christians. If privileges are provided to *dalits* belonging to non-Christian religious traditions why it is not furnished to Christian *dalits*? Prejudice in the name of religion is as worse on the prejudice in the name of caste system.

The *dalits* are the oppressed, marginated and the voiceless people of India. Anyone who is oppressed is a '*Dalit*' in the broad sense of the term. Since the so called low caste people are oppressed and crushed ruthlessly by the dominant, the term '*dalit*' is referred specifically in relation to them. They are socially weak, economically backward and politically powerless. The caste system has contributed to the pathetic, condition of the *dalits*. They are, now, away from the mainstream of the society. Historically they were alienated for more than five thousand years. This Dravidian community which is scattered in different parts of India as a result of Aryan suppression, is struggling to come up.

Around fifteen per cent of the *dalits* in India are Christians. It is also observed that around three-fourth of the Christians in India are *dalits*. The *dalit* Christians are thrice oppressed. They are being oppressed by the society, the church and the government. The Simon Commission 1927 had summarized the demands of *dalits* to include (1) adequate representation for *dalits* in local, provincial and central legislatures, (2) extension of franchise and (3) safeguarding their education and civil right. Dr B.R. Ambedkar has considered *dalits* as a separate minority from Hindu community. The question before the Simon Commission was whether Christian *dalits* should be considered separately or not. The All India Adi-Dravida Jana Sabha argued that the dalit can be a depressed one even after becoming a Christian after conversion. It should be asserted that whether Hindu or Christian *dalits* are depressed so religion should not be 'a barrier to consider' them as scheduled castes. We find discrimination in the constitution itself which goes against the vision of the preamble that affirms the equality, liberty and justice of all, regardless of caste and religion. The Articles 14 and 15 of the Constitution do not accept any kinds of discrimination on the ground of religion, race, caste, sex and place of birth.

It is surprising to note that the Government of India Act, 1935 argues that no Indian Christian shall be declared as scheduled caste. The Constitution has been amended several times to define the scheduled caste. In 1950, the Constitution (Article 341 — which empowered the President to form a list of scheduled castes) explained that only Hindus are scheduled castes and no other. In 1960, it is defined that the Sikhs, the Jainists and Buddhist can also be recognized as 'Hindu' and they should be included in the scheduled caste list. It is interesting to note that our Constitution has recognized the *dalit* converts to Jainism, Buddhism and Sikhism as Hindu and failed to recognize, the *dalit* converts, to Christianity. This discrimination goes against the, secularist ideals of our Constitution. What the Christian *dalits* demand is not to recognize them as Hindus, but to consider them as scheduled castes to have their constitutional rights and privileges.

The *dalit* Christians are an oppressed group of people along with all other *dalits*. So they should get their privileges in the area of employment, education and economic assistance which will enhance their social mobility. Whether Christians, Hindus or Sikhs, the *dalits* are dalits and they are being oppressed. So the *dalit* Christians should also be constitutionally protected. In the struggle of the *dalit* Christians to get their constitutional privileges, all the *dalits* should unite. The cause of the *dalit* Christians is the cause of all *dalits*. Sad to say, certain Hindu *dalit* organizations are protesting against the inclusion of *dalit* Christians in the scheduled caste list. All *dalits* have to unite in the struggle for their justice or human rights.

Tribals and Human Rights

The tribals are indigenous group of people who are referred as *Adivasis*. They are also known as *Girijans*. A consultation group of the representations of tribal committees met in Shillong in 1962 described the 'tribe as an indigenous, homogeneous unit, speaking a common language, claiming a common ancestry, living in a particular geographical area, backward in technology, pre-literate loyally observing social and political customs based on kinship' (M.M Thomas and Richard W. Taylor; *Tribal Awakening*, pp.2-3). Tribals are living together in a particular territory having their own distinct culture or way of life and a common ancestry. The major tribal groups are around 414.

The tribes of India are distributed in three geographical areas:

(a) Those living in northern and north-eastern India, mostly in the mountains and valleys, and the Eastern Frontiers of India.
(b) Those occupying the central belt of the older hills and plateaus along the dividing line between the Indo-Gangetic plain and peninsular India.
(c) Those scattered over south-western India, in the hills and the converging lines of the ghats (*Tribal Awakening,* pp.5-6).

The tribals are the exploited and oppressed. Gramsci called them subalterns. Dr. Walter Fernandes noted that "when the Constitution of India completed, Dr. B.R. Ambedkar rejoiced that it has ensured political democracy, i.e., one person one vote. But he added that only political equality is of no avail without social, economic and cultural freedom. The last 50 years of independence have proved him right. The social, political cultural and economic structures and the pattern of development have combined so further strengthen the already strong and weaken the powerless" ("The cry of the marginalized: set us free" *Faith Theological Review*, Vol. III, Nos. 1 & 2, 1999, p.1).

P.D. Mathew states, the following acts committed by a person, who does not belong to the Scheduled Castes or Scheduled Tribes are considered as the offences or atrocities, by the Scheduled Castes and Scheduled Tribes (Prevention of Atrocities) Act, 1989 :

(i) Forcing a member of a Scheduled Caste or Scheduled Tribe to eat any inedible (uneatable) or obnoxious substance (hurtful matter).

(ii) Dumping excreta, waste matter, carcasses (dead body) or any obnoxious (hurtful/disgusting) substance in his premises or neighbourhood with the intention of causing him insult or annoyance.

(iii) Forcefully removing the clothes of a Scheduled Caste/ Scheduled Tribe person and parading him/her naked or with painted face or body or doing any similar act derogatory to human dignity.

(iv) Illegally occupying or cultivating any land owned by or alloted to a Scheduled Caste/Scheduled Tribe person.

(v) Illegally transferring any land allotted to a Scheduled Caste/Scheduled Tribe person to any other person.

(vi) Illegally evicting a Scheduled Caste/Scheduled Tribe person from his land or premises or interfering with the use of land, water or premises.

(vii) Compelling or forcing a Scheduled Caste/Scheduled Tribe person to do begar (forced labour) or other similar forms of forced or bonded labour prohibited by law.

(viii) Preventing a Scheduled Caste/Scheduled Tribe person from voting or forcing him/her to vote for a particular candidate or vote in a manner prohibited by law.

(ix) Instituting a false suit or criminal proceeding against a Scheduled Caste/Scheduled Tribe person.

(x) Giving false information to any public servant and thereby compelling him to use his power to cause injury, harm or harassment to a Scheduled Caste/ Scheduled Tribe person.

(xi) Insulting or intimidating a Scheduled Caste/Scheduled Tribe person in public with the intention of humiliating that person.

(xii) Dishonouring or outraging the modesty of any woman belonging to a Scheduled Caste/Scheduled Tribe.

(xiii) Using any custodial or authoritative position to exploit (sexually) a woman belonging to a Scheduled Caste/ Scheduled Tribe.

(xiv) Polluting the water of a spring or reservoir ordinarily used by members of Scheduled Castes/Scheduled Tribes so as to make it unfit for use.

(xv) Denying a Scheduled Caste/Scheduled Tribe person a customary right of passage to a public resort or preventing him/her from using it.

(xvi) Forcing a Scheduled Caste/Scheduled Tribe person to leave his/her house or village.

A convicted person can be punished with imprisonment of minimum six months and maximum five years and with fine (P.D. Mathew, *The Law on Atrocities against Scheduled Castes and Scheduled Tribes*, pp.3-4).

The tribals are alienated and their resources are tapped, but their rights are not recognized. They are evacuated from their habitats in the name of development and when they challenges the oppression they are stamped as anti-nationals. Around ten lakh tribals are evacuated from Narmada valley. Their rights over the land is not accepted. In the Jharkhand region the tribals struggle for their autonomy. The territorial integrity and autonomy are the two major concerns of tribals which are the significant rights of these people. Displacement in a serious human rights violation for the tribals as they live by the forests and their resources. It is actually chasing away the tribals as they are not having rights over the land. According to Walter Fernandes, "Displacement is a basic issue in the resource rich tribal areas. Their plight has also to be situated in the context of the absence of an official database on the members affected till now. According to one estimate, at least 213 lakh persons have been displaced of otherwise deprived of their livelihood by development schemes between 1951 and 1990" (*Faith Theological Review*, Vol. III, No. 142, p.24).

Uprooting the tribals from their habitat is against their rights as they cannot live in the other social settings. In most of the new situations they are economically exploited and so also the tribal women are sexually exploited. They undergo severe crisis socially and psychologically and economically. So it is important to help them to develop in their own territory. They should be given more participation in the political structure and should not reduce them as vote banks. According to Wati Longchar, the tribal people struggle for identity, justice and participation. Their history in full of defeat, subjugation, genocide, exploitation, discrimination, displacement and alienation. They are cheated, dehumanized, bonded labourers in their own land resources are exploited and their dignity is not accepted ["Tribal theology: Issues, method and perspective", *Journal of Tribal Studies,* Vol. IV, No.2 (July-December 2000) p.75].

R.J.K. Kootoom writes, "many unfortunate tribes have already taken farewell from the world. Civilization has squeezed them out of this world. The rest are facing a serious threat of extinction or a life of slavery. Our big brothers want us to be their coolies; when we refused, they plan to finish us. Ruthless exploitation, deprivation from human rights, alienation from land, suppression of our ethnic identity and derogation of our culture and traditions have been almost paralyzing us" [quoted by Wati Longchar in *Journal of Tribal Studies,* Vol. IV, No.2 (July-Dec. 2000), p.47].

According to Jagnath Pathy, the tribals are vulnerable to gross violations of fundamental human rights, including being victim of physical aggression, persecution, brutal repression and blatant discriminations [*Religion and Society*,

Vol. XXXXVIII, Nos. 3 & 4, (Sept.-Dec. 1991), p.24]. The tribal peoples are referred as primitive, savage and uncivilized which are very derogatory and question the basic right as a human. A working Group on indigenous peoples (WIGIP) was installed to formulate a proposal for United Nations Declaration on the Rights of the indigenous peoples. The first draft (1988) endorsed the call for promotion of indigenous societies, cultures and traditions through ethno-development, and comprehensive participation, recognized their inalienable rights to decide their own future development" (*Ibid.*, p.26).

The *Adivasis* demand their right over land. "They demand autonomy and equality, conserving the environment and right to over the natural resources of their world, collectively", says C.R. Bijoy (*Ibid.*, p.35). The Jharkhand movement is understood by the tribals as their right to regain self-determination, says Bosu Mullick (*Ibid.*, p.39). They struggle for autonomy. He points out that they lost their communal rights over means of production, collective leadership and principle of consensus in the decision-making process, equitable status of men and women and the ethical life.

The *Adivasis* land struggle in Kerala is a historical event. Kerala has 3.2 lakh *Adivasis* constituting 1.10 per cent of the total population. The Kerala Scheduled Tribes (Restriction of Transfer of Lands and Restoration of Lands) Act, 1975, was erected as Act 31 of 1975, and was included in the 9th schedule to ensure that the Act itself should not be challenged in the court of law. The Act was passed in 1986 with retrospective effect from 1960. The Act makes all transactions of *Adivasi* lands during the period 1960 to 1982 invalid and to be restored by the state back to the original owners, who will have to pay a sum as compensation, which is the total of the amount received, if any, and, as determined by authorities, the amount spent for improvement on the land since the transaction. The government may advance this required sum to the *Adivasi* beneficiary of the

Act as loan, which is to repaid in 20 years. The Act restricts the transfer of *Adivasi* lands to non-*Advasis* from 1982 without the consent of authorities ["Adivasi Land Struggles in Kerala", *People's Reporter* (December 1-15, 1994), p.4].

The *Adivasi* question is not of welfare and charity but of restoring their income generating resources, namely the land. The government machinery, bureaucracy and the politicians support the elites and the land issue is not taken seriously. Interests of the dominant are served by our social and political system so the rights of the original inhabitants are denied. So they live as marginated and victims of injustice. However, the *Adivasis* are more organized today to gain their rights.

The Rights of Fisherfolk

Fisherfolk is one of the most marginated groups who struggled to survive meaningfully. They are affected by the climatic situations, the competition from the mechanized boats and also from the rich and dominant on whom they depend. The trawling is challenging the traditional fisherfolk who use small boats or 'catamarams' (boat made by binding two or three big pieces of wood). Though restrictions are made by law that the seashore fishing is not permitted to mechanized boats they violate the rules and even engage in fighting with fisherfolk who have traditional boats.

Sea is the resource of the fisherfolk. They live by the sea so their right over this means of living is to be protected. In the breeding season of fishes, the mechanized boats violate the regulations and spoil the eggs. The pursuits nets could even cause damage to eggs which results in ecological disaster. The fish resource can be diminished and the means of living of the traditional fisherfolk can be lost. The poor fisherfolk is affected badly but the rich business lobby is gaining much out of the human right violations.

The fisherfolk constitutes the *dalits* or the poor. It is significant to emancipate them from the clutches of business lobbies. The education of their children, health care and their welfare are quite significant in relation to their rights. It is important to curb the intrusion of the mechanized boats and also the foreign fishing ships. The world forum of fisher peoples is an organization that work for the rights of the fisherfolk. It is an organization of traditional fisherfolk and those who involve in small-scale fishing. About the fisherfolk unions in India, Fr. Aloysius D.Fernandes states, "The work style of the unions, the federation and the national forum has turned very much struggling for their rights than for welfare measures, although welfare-measure demands were also there" [*Faith Theological Review,* Vol. III, Nos. 1 & 2 (March & September, 1999), p.6].

Living with dignity is the right of the fisherfolk. The fisherfolk is neglected as illiterate and uncivilized and their cry is not heard. Their voice is not given importance as the structure of the dominant crush them. They are an oppressed community. Socially, they are deprived, politically powerless and they are merely the vote banks of the political parties. Their empowerment and upholding the rights are not very much the concern of government and the society. Exploiting the fisher people is the prime motive of the society and not to uplift them. The fisherfolk of the third world is struggling to live with dignity, and their living conditions are pathetic. The affirmation of their rights should be the foremost concern.

Jesus was very much aware of the struggles of the fisherfolk. They were the active members of Jesus' community. He loved them and identified with them. He accepted their dignity and affirmed their humanity. He joined them in fishing when we knew that they did not get any catch. He was compassionate as he come to know their desperate condition.

The fisherfolk was the most marginated people of the time,

but Jesus found disciples among them. It is important for the church to identify with them and to work for their rights.

The Eco-Rights

The rights from the perspective of ecology is significant in this respect. Our environment is undergoing crisis because of water, soil and air pollutions. The major contribution to this crisis is from the rash use of science and technology. The industrialization is an important reason to this crisis. The chemical waste from the factories pollute the atmosphere so also the emission of carbo fluro oxides and carbon monoxide. The radioactive waste is dumped into the rivers and oceans which make life difficult. These bring threat to humanity, plant kingdom and animal kingdom which is a violation of environmental or eco-rights.

The ruthless development leads to depletion of resources and threat to life. The rights of *dalits* and tribals are violated in the name of development. The resources are tapped without any discernment. The deforestation also contribute to ecological crisis. According to Winin Pereira, rights to natural resources and a clean environment should automatically accrue from the right to life (*Inhuman Rights*, p.69). He continued to say that if all human beings are born equal in rights then all people now living on the globe and all who will be born in the future have equal rights to the earth's resources' (*Ibid.*, p.70). He points out that hyper consumption is also a violation of human rights. He states, "Hyper consumption by a small section of the global population deprives others of their rights" (*Ibid.*, p.70). According to Vandana Shiva, "the ecological consequence of western science and technology involve a violation of rights to resources as a human right" (*Human Wrongs*, p.152). Control over seeds and the patent laws are the violations of farmer's rights. Multinationals abduct the rights of the farmers from the third world.

Vandana Shiva opines, "The destruction of the planet's

resources for the heavy resource demands of western-style technological development goes hand in hand with violation of ecological rights as a human right. Whether it is the anti-dam movements in Narmada valley or Tehri, or the movements against shrimp farming and deep sea fishing, or the seed *satyagraha* launched by Indian farmers, the tribals, peasants and fisherfolk fighting to protect the land and the sea, the trees and seeds, are not just protecting nature. They perceive their struggle as human rights struggle to defend their livelihoods, life-styles, and life support systems. The protection of the environment and their human rights converge; they are not divergent" (*Ibid.*, p.163).

The issues like Greenhouse effect, acid rains as a result of global warming are severe ecological problems so also the toxic waste. Another serious problem is the nuclear power. A. Pushparajan states, "In the wake of severe energy crisis all over the world some western countries claimed that generation of power through fission and fusion of atoms would be viable solution. Least do people realize the serious difficulties involved in production of nuclear energy. The most formidable of the difficulties is about the disposal of radioactive waste which occur during fission of atoms. It is not possible to devise safe enough containers to store such wastes. For, plutonium, the most poisonous of all radioactive products remains toxic for at least 5,00,000 years". ("Towards eco-spirituality and environmental ethics for the church in India" *in Towards an ecological world view for the Mission of the church,* edited by Bennet Benjamin, p.21). It is realised that it is 20,000 times more toxic than cobra venom or potassium cyanide and it causes cancer. It violates the rights of living beings to live meaningful in this universe.

When we talk about ecological crises it affects the women badly and the most. The water scarcity, water pollution, depletion of resources, deforestation, evacuation from the habitat, and the whole violence against creation is a violence against women as they suffer a lot because of these. According to Aruna Guanadasan, "women suffer the most when clean water, fuel and healthy clean surroundings are not available. Women know what the shortage of water means they know how the health of their families are affected when the environment they live in is not safe" (*Towards an ecological world view for the mission of the church*, p.29). Violation of environmental rights is the violation of women's rights. This is where eco-feminism has a dominant role to play. The *chipko* movement in the Uttarakhand region of the Himalayas (it was a tribal women-centred struggle, women, children and men had clung to the trees in order to protect them from the saws of the contractors' men or in their struggle against mining operation in the mountain region) need a special mention here in this regard.

Fidel Castro observes about the West that, "with only 20 per cent of the world's population, they consume two-thirds of all metals and three-fourths of the energy produced worldwide. They have poisoned the seas and rivers. They have polluted the air. They have weakened and perforated the ozone layer. They have saturated the atmosphere with gases, altering climatic conditions with the catastrophic effects we are already beginning to suffer" (*Tomorrow is too late*, p.3). According to his view human kind is an endangered species. The forests disappear and deserts expand, billions of tons of fertile soil are washed every year into the sea and numerous species are becoming extinct (*Ibid.*, p.1). Here the main issue is about the right of the whole creation to survive. We are not supposed to exploit the creation, but to deal fairly with it. Justice should be done to the whole of creation as we care and protect them.

In India certain rules are enacted to prevent the ecological problems. There was Water (Prevention and Control of Pollution) Cess Act, 1977 and Air Pollution Act. The latest one is the

Environment (Protection) Act, 1986. This Act defines environmental pollutant as any solid, liquid or gaseous substance which cause injury to environment. It also talks about hazardous substance (chemicals) which harms human beings, other living creatures, plants, micro organisms, property or environment. The Indian Penal Code (sections 268-290) dealing with public nuisance which include the action that causes danger, obstruction, injury or annoyance to the public or any other hazardous activities (P.D. Mathew, P.M. Bakshi, *Ensuring a safe environment: Laws against pollution,* pp.1ff). The eco-right is very much to be stressed for the survival of the humanity and the whole creation. Eco-right in a basic right for all living creatures.

Rights of Minorities

Minorities are of two kinds—linguistic minorities and religious minorities. The Constitution of India guarantees right to equality to every citizen of India (Articles 14-18). Article 15 rejects any discrimination in the name of religion, race or caste. All minorities (Christians, Muslims, Parsees) are given the right of freedom of conscience, the right to profess, practice and propagate religion by the Constitution (Articles 25-28). The religious and linguistic minorities are having the right to establish and administer [Article 30(1)] educational institutions of their choice. It affirms the choice of the minority to establish educational institutions to serve the purpose of conserving their religion, language or culture and also the purpose of giving through general education to their children in their own language. Article 30(2) provides that the state shall not, in granting aid to educational institutions, discriminate against any educational institution on the ground that it is under the management of a minority, whether based on religion or language (J.N. Pandey, *Constitutional Law of India,* p.227). Article 29(1) guarantees the rights of minorities to conserve their language, script or culture.

The Minorities Commission was established by the Central Government by a resolution dated January 12, 1978 to safeguard the interest of minorities. Most of the states also instituted Minorities Commission (K.S. Durrany, *State Measures for the welfare of minorities,* pp.5ff).

The religious minorities undergo severe crises in Indian context today. The Hinduva ideology comes strong to oppress the minorities in the name of religion. Though the Constitution of India safeguards the rights of the Christians and Muslims, the fundamentalist forces question the secularism. They try to enforce the R.S.S. agenda to chase the religious minorities away from Indian soil. Articles 25-28 of Indian Constitution provides the right to freedom of religion.

One of the major debate the recent time is on conversion. The persecution is also going on in different parts of India by Hindu fundamentalists over the minorities like Christians and Muslims. The right to believe in any other religion or ideology other than 'Hindu' is in question in India today. The Aryanization or saffronization is the aim of the Hindu fanatics. They appear as the custodians of Hindu culture and religion. They believe that Indian culture is an Aryan culture, though Dravidian culture is pre-Aryan and a dominant culture. The right to profess and propagate one's religion is challenged and the right to freedom of religion is challenged. They challenge the secular nature of our country. They like India to be a mono-religious country than religiously pluralistic.

Indian Constitution is formed on the pillar of secularism. Article 25(1) guarantees to every person the freedom of conscience and the right to profess, practice and propagate religion. This right is subject to public order and morality. The freedom of conscience is absolute inner freedom of citizen to mould his own relation with God. To profess a religion means to declare freely and openly one's faith and belief. To practice religion indicate that to perform the prescribed religious duties, rites and rituals. To propagate means to spread and publicize one's own religion. No one is permitted to use fraud means such as force or allurement to change one's religion (J.N. Pandey, *Constitutional Law of India*, p.214).

Arunachal Pradesh (1978), Madhya Pradesh (1968) and Orissa (1978) erected their own Freedom of Religion Acts. These Acts are meant to curtail freedom of religion. Forcible conversions are prohibited by these Acts, but in fact it questions all the conversions to another religion, especially to Christianity, [Mathai Zacheriah (ed.) *Freedom of Religion in India*, p.3ff]. There is severe violence towards Christianity from these states. Christian churches are burnt and Christian missionaries are chased out or killed. Human right violations are so severe in these states. Graham Staines and his sons Timothy and Philip were mercilessly killed by the Hindu fanatics. Staines family was effectively serving the leprosy patients in the state of Orissa.

Many fundamentalist forces tried to reconvert the tribals and other Christians to Hinduism by means of Shuddhi (purification ceremony), accusing that these people are converted to Christianity by force or allurement. These are real evidences for human right violations which are, however, not accounted by. There is a strong bias towards Christianity and Islam by the Hindu fundamentalist forces.

10

HUMAN RIGHTS
Specific Issues

Rights of Children

It is estimated that the working children in our country are 44 million. 80,000 to 100,000 children are working in Kashmiri carpet industry. It is calculated that about 45,000 children work in match and fire work factories in Sivakasi and become victims of exploitation. 92 million children in India exist below the poverty line and they are malnourished [K.C. Abraham (ed.) *Cry for life*, p.8]. The children work in hotels, factories and shops with inadequate wages.

The conditions of the girl children are more tragic than the boy children. They are ill-treated by the family members as their dignity is questioned and they are sexually exploited and also malnourished. The children work over time in factories and draw very low wages. A number of children including girl children, are rag pickers. Sharmila Joshi states that domestic workers are not fed properly. One eleven year old is given a cup of tea every morning without sugar and her meals are meagre. Malnutrition, hardwork and poor access to medical facilities result in several illness, like anemia, skin infections and stomach cramps (*The Unseen Worker*, p.25).

It is found that migrant children are often sexually abused. Tourists sexually molest these children. Child prostitution is reported to be rampant in Goa. Several minors are used in this act. Most of these children are forcibly brought to "enhance" or "develop" tourism. These are to be curbed as it promotes evil and are violating the rights and dignity of children.

Indian Constitution (Article 24) prohibits employment of children below 14 years of age in factories and hazardous employment. The Children Labour (Prohibition and Regulation) Act in 1989 regulates employment of children and totally bans it only in 25 hazardous processes and occupations, including beedi-making, tanning, carpet-weaving and making fire crackers (*The Unseen Worker*, p.40).

The South Asian Association for Regional Corporation (SAARC) declared a year and decade of the girl child (1990 and 1991-2000). The Government of India announced a national plan of action for the girl child, 1991-2000. United Nations Convention on the rights of the child was held on 1989 (it does not specifically mention the girl child). UN's fourth world conference on women (1995) deal with girl child (*Assignment : Giving voice to the unheard*, p.1). A girl child is internationally defined as a human being below the age of 18.

Infant mortality death is very high in India. UNICEF publication *Glimpses of Girlhood in India* states that about a quarter of the approximately 12 million girls born in India every year do not survive to see their 15th birthday. The health problems, malnutrition parental bias (in Uslampatti, near Madurai where it is found that girl children are poisoned to death because of economic burdens like dowry) towards girl children are causing their death. It is also observed that girl infants are breast fed less frequently than boys. There is discrimination in the food allocation to girl child.

About the rights of children United Nations Declaration on Human Rights [Article 25(x)] states, "Motherhood and childhood are entitled to special care and assistance. All children, whether born in or out of wedlock, shall enjoy the same social protection." The UN Convention on Rights of the Child was adopted by the assembly in 1989 as follows :

(a) The right to survival includes the right to life, the highest attainable standard of health, nutrition and adequate standard of living.
(b) The right to protection which includes freedom from all forms of exploitation, abuse, inhuman or degrading treatment, and neglect including the right to special protection in situations of emergency and armed conflicts.
(c) The right to development which includes right to education, support for early childhood development and care, social security, and the right to leisure, recreation and cultural activities.
(d) The right to participation which includes respect for the views of the child, freedom of expression, access to appropriate information, and freedom of thought, conscience and religion (*Inhuman Rights*, pp.137-138).

Any discrimination to children in the area of education opportunities and participation, sex, food and freedom of expression are human right violations.

Right to Information

Right to information is an essential right of human beings. When something goes wrong, people demand the government to publish a white paper to know the facts. Right to know is people's right. In the area of medical ethics also, it is a significant issue. The patients have the right to know the result of diagnosis, the whereabouts of the diseases about the treatment and its effects. The producers use to hide the bad effects of medicines or any other products. The industries also keep in secret the consequences of the processes. Emission of pollutants like Carbondioxide and carbon-fluro-oxides are usually not informed to the public. In the field of banking also this danger is found. They usually talk about advantages and do not reveal the risk factors. This is a great deception and violation of human right. According toWinin Pereira "people are rarely informed of all the possible environmental, health or impoverishing and culturally damaging effects flowing from any policy, product or activity" (*Inhuman Rights,* p.132).

Right to Communicate

Freedom of speech and freedom of press are the important areas in this respect. Freedom of speech and expression in found is Articles 19(1) and 19(2). Article 19(1)(a) says that all citizens shall have the right to freedom of speech and expression. Article 19(2) which empowers the state to put 'reasonable' restrictions on the following grounds, e.g. security of the state, friendly relations with foreign states, public order, decency and morality, contempt of court, defamation, incitement to offence and integrity and sovereignty of India. According to Dr. J.N. Pandey, "freedom of speech and expression means the right to express one's own convictions and opinions freely by words of mouth, writing, printing, pictures or any other mode. It thus includes the expression of one's ideas through any communicable medium or visible representation, such as gesture, signs and the like" (*Constitutional Law of India*, p.126).

Media and Human Rights

The means of communication includes the newspapers, magazines, journals, radio, television, cinema, computer disc, (CD) and Website. Media can play a vital role to rise the conscience of the people against what is evil and unjust. Unfortunately media is used by the dominant to fulfil their purpose. Reality is distorted and what is immoral is projected by these means. The advertisements give a wrong picture of woman. Private parts of their body are projected in the name of advertisements. Some advertisements are discriminate towards *dalits* and tribals.

The movies/films give pictures of violence as an adventure, or sex which provides an 'ideal' to the watchers. What they have seen in the movies affect badly the perspectives of the watchers. The sex and violence are understood to be the ways in which the people could be manipulated to watch the film and by that the produces could make money. Commercial motives are behind cinema which undermines the morality.

It is the matter of those who controls the media. The reports, news or facts are hidden by some media as they represent contain ideology or worldview. The newspapers and TV channels which represent certain religious and secular ideologies present the facts favouring their stance and they hide the facts or do not report the facts if it is not favouring them. Objectivity is not upheld by them. These can be said as unjust or not right. The gender discrimination is quite evident in the media. Morphing is very common in the media sphere. Nude pictures of women are inserted in the Website. Women become an object of entertainment for at least a group of people. They are objectified for their pleasure, commercial purpose and monetary gains.

Media should have a prophetic role to play. Media should safeguard the interest of the marginated and it has to involve in conscientization. Creating awareness on human rights is its obligation.

Science, Technology and Human Rights

From the ecological perspective, the role of science and technology has been discussed in this book. But here the perspective is very general in character. According to B.D. Nag Chaudhari, Science and technology are like a couple of spiritual horses. They are useful and necessary to travel for a described future. But they are to be kept under full control otherwise it can bring disaster. It is very evident that the science and technology should have a human face to serve the humanity. Science should not be used for destructive purposes.

Thorium is widely used in nuclear reactors, so there is radioactive wastes and even leakage which are so hazardous. Japan is still suffering from the radioactive elements because of the American bombing in the second world war. Chernobyl (erstwhile Soviet Russia) is doing harm to thousands of people because of the leakage. The Pokhran nuclear tests in India affects so many people though the authorities are silent on the issue and forcing 'Buddha to laugh'. The whole atmosphere is polluted by the radioactive elements and it is a danger to humanity.

The capital intensive technology cannot help the poor to come up. The present model of industrial development, computerisation and agricultural production will help only the affluent minority. A system that is regulated by the dominant will only favour the dominant and it does not consider the welfare of the marginated. Greed has contributed to disturb ecological systems that grass lands become deserts, lakes and rivers have dried, and vast agricultural lands become dust bowls.

The science and technology should ensure peoples

participation and it should help to alleviate the poverty and also to meet the basic needs of the poor. What happens today is that the Indian elites and western capitalists collaborate in transfer of technology so they would be benefited out of it. Technology should be to uphold the rights of the poor as to safeguard their need and interests. The more appropriate technology in Indian set-up is to be labour-using, capital and energy-saving and small scale. Science and technology should help to humanize the living conditions of people. The ethical commitment is quite essential for scientists and technocrats to develop systems which are serving the good of the poor.

Science and Technology do sometimes act irresponsibly. This is very clear in the area of human life — irresponsible abortions/foeticide, cloning, the experiments on human body, artificial means to overcome infertility and euthanasia. Corruption in the form of manipulation can become inhuman as it violates the rights of humans. Persons are objectified and scientists could hide the facts from persons to "fulfil their purpose". Euthanasia can be applied without the knowledge of the person in subtle manners by them which is also a human right violation. Science should have openness, sense of love and justice in order to uphold the human right. (Refer, *Science for Sane Societies,* Madras: CLS, 1980 and *Science and our future,* Madras : CLS, 1978, by Paulos Mar Gregorios).

11

HUMAN RIGHT MOVEMENTS

The human right is considered by some organizations as their main focus. Amnesty International is a voluntary organization which work on behalf of people detained because of their beliefs, colour, sex, ethnic origin, language or religion. In India, 'Vigil India Movement' is an organization which stand for the cause of human rights. It challenges the black laws and other developments which are non-democratic, inhuman and against what is secular. In Europe several human right organizations were emerged— 'The European Conventions for the Protection of Human Rights' (1950), 'The European Commission on Human Rights' (1953), 'European Court of Human Rights' (1958), 'The Amnesty International' (1961). It should be noted that 1968 was the International year for human rights.

Besides these, there are many organizations or action groups work for the rights of the women, *dalits*, tribals, blacks, poor and for the cause of ecology. The Civil Rights movement led by Martin Luther King Jr. in North America worked for the liberation of the blacks. They obtained their rights as citizens of America—the freedom to exercise franchise, right to employment and freedom of movement. 'Ella Baker Centre for Human Rights' in United States stand for the rights of the blacks. Ella Baker was involved in the Civil Rights movement led by Martin Luther King Jr. It organizes the blacks for the atrocities done against them by police. The independent movement of Fisherfolk (Swatantra Matsyathozhilali Union) of Kerala is a movement for the rights of the fisherfolk. Vimochana is an organization in India which stand for the human rights. They use folk medias like street plays to conscientize the people of their rights in the context of oppression.

In India, 'The National Human Rights Commission' (NHRC) was established in 1993 which defines human rights as the rights relating to life, liberty and dignity of persons. The chipko movement (Uttar Pradesh/ Uttarakhand) and Appiko movement (Karnataka) stand for the ecological concerns. The trees are protected by women from deforestation. The tribal women were active in these ecological movements. The 'Narmada Valley Andolan' is another ecological movement spearheaded by Baba Amte and Medha Patkar. The green peace movement is also safeguarding the eco-rights. The ecological awareness is created by them. It is a worldwide movement.

Women movements are also strong in India. 'Sthreevedi' is a movement for the rights of women, so also *Manushi* a magazine which stands for women's rights. There is another movement which is 'Anveshi'. 'Forum of Christian women for women's rights' work to create awareness among women and fight for the right of women. The mine workers of Madhya Pradesh organized themselves as 'Mahila Mukti Morcha'. 'Gethkari' is an organization of peasants in Maharashtra. 'All India Women's Conference' was found before the independence of India, which stood for self- sufficiency in economy, educational opportunities and equality.

'All India Democratic Women's Association' stand for the rights of women. It challenges the exploitation, inequality and gender discrimination towards women.

The *dalit* organizations for rights are also important. '*Dalit* Christian Federation', 'Christian Dalit Liberation Movement' are Christian *dalit* movements. There are other movements like Dalit Panthers, All India Adidravida Mahajana Sabha, All India Depressed Classes Conference and Republican Party. They try to organize the *dalits* and work for their rights.

12

HUMAN RIGHTS
Sources and Reflections

M.M. Thomas

He identified three fundamental elements in India's revolution: (1) right to bread, (2) right to dignity, (3) right of every group and person to spiritual self-determination.

He advocated the militancy of the urban and rural poor to assert their rights against oppression and exploitation. He argued for co-operation with men of all religions and no religion to humanize the contemporary social and political revolution in India, to criticize and protest against the structures of politics of state, so that they may serve men, to enhance his dignity and uphold his rights. He emphasized the need to generate to all individual citizens' freedom of religions and to all religious minority groups their legitimate religious and secular rights.

When Mrs. Indira Gandhi the former Prime Minister of India declared emergency on 25th June, 1975, M.M. Thomas stood against that tyranny.

(a) He argued for the freedom of expression and stood against the suppression of civil liberties.

(b) Argued for the legitimate rights of the opposition in democracy.

(c) Fought against 'Maintenance of Internal Security Act' (MISA) which was a real violation of human right of the citizens.

Human Rights and Human Development

The Human Development Report, 2000 stated that poverty eradication is not just a development goal but the central concern for human rights. It is asserted that poverty eradication is a major human rights challenge of the new century. Poverty limits human freedom and deprives a person of dignity. Decent standard of living, adequate nutrition, health care, education, decent work and protection against calamities are not development goals — they are also human rights (*People's Reporter*, July 10-25, 2000, p.6).

Thomas Jefferson

Thomas Jefferson (1743-1826) was the third President of the United States of America. He was almost wholly responsible for the "Original Rough Draft" of the declaration of independence of thirteen American colonies from Great Britain. It states, "We hold these truths to be sacred and unalienable, that all men are created equal and independent, that from that equal creation they derive rights inherent and inalienable, among which are the preservation of life, and liberty, and the pursuit of happiness; that to secure these ends governments are instituted among men, deriving their just powers from the consent of the governed; that whenever any form of government shall become destructive of these ends, it is the right of the people to alter or to abolish it, and to institute new government, laying its foundation on such principles and organizing its powers to such format, as to them principles and organizing its powers to such format, as to them shall seem most likely to effect them safety will dictate that governments long established should not changed for light and transient causes: and accordingly all experience hath shown that mankind are most disposed to suffer while evils are sufferable, than to right themselves by abolishing the forms to which they are accustomed. But when a long train of abuses and usurpation begun at a distinguished period and pursuing invariably the same subject evinces a design to subject them to arbitrary power, it is their right, it is their duty, to throw off such government and to provide new guards for their future safety. (*Themes for Living-society* by Geoffrey Parrinder, Amersham, Hulton Educational Publications Ltd., 1973, p.51).

On conversion debate

Philip D'Souza said the following in an article "Foreign faith, homegrown hated", *Times of India*, Mumbai, 17-1-99. "After a day in Gujarat's Dangs district, our Prime Minister (A.B. Vajpayee) calls for a "National debate" on conversions because they are the "root" of the problems there. Now surely the root of the trouble is the pitiful state of the tribals, in Dangs and elsewhere. Surely the national debate we must urgently have is about how hundreds of millions of us live deprived lives, how that alone so cripples India. Surely that is the more pressing issue than a few hundred or a few thousand, a few lakh, whatever it is conversion a year" (P.D. Mathew, 'Freedom of Religion and a "Debate" on Religious Conversion', p.76).

Right to survival in the basic right

Here is a comment by Kalindi Mazumdar on female foeticide which is a violation of human right. She says "this is a very basic right indeed and logically there should be no controversy in relation to this right. In reality, however, the struggle for survival continues throughout the woman's life beginning with the female foetus. The advent of amniocentesis in India has given yet another blow to this struggle." She continues to state, "In fact amniocentesis is propagated through advertisements which influence the psychology of parents. For instance in Delhi there are advertisements such as "pay Rs. 500 now or Rs. 5 lakhs later (dowry)". In Bombay, an abortion costs Rs. 60 it is estimated that between 1978 and 1983 as many as 78,000 female foetuses in India have been aborted". ("Woman and violence: A human Rights perspective", *Violence Against Woman: Woman Against Violence,* p.29).

A critique of rights by Catherine MacKinnon

Nivedita Menon says: "A powerful and influential critique of rights, law and the state has come from Catherine MacKinnon who argues that liberalism supports state intervention on behalf of women as abstract persons with abstract rights while in reality 'the state is male in feminist sense'. Abstract rights only 'authorize the male experience of the world'. As a result, she holds feminist understandings of the world have been 'Schizoid'—on the one hand recognizing the world as patriarchal and oppressive and on the other, turning to the law to make the lawless sexist. She sees the state as embodying and ensuring male control over female sexuality even while it juridically prohibits excesses" ("Rights, law and feminist politics: Rethinking our practice", *In the Name of Justice: Woman and Law in Society,* p.17).

The plight of the dalits and their liberation

Poornam Daemel states, "The Dalit Christians' liberation does not mean acquiring peripheral rights like sitting in the church or reservations from the state. These may be necessary inasmuch as they contribute to the total and integral liberation of Dalit Christians as humans. This in praxis means a radical restructuring of power relations" ("Dalit Christian experiences", *Emerging Dalit Theology*, edited by Xavier Irudayaraj, Madurai: Jesuit Theological Secretariate, 1990, p.33).

Dr. Franklyn J. Balasundaram on the Dalits

He states, "The Indian Government has consistently maintained that India does not have indigenous people. This is being considered as an upper caste conspiracy against dalits (also Tribals) and a direct denial of the existence and identity of our 300 million Dalits. This is certainly a violation of Human Right and a direct genocide of the dalits" ["Set us free— A cry of the marginalized Dalit perspective", *Faith Theological Review*, Vol. III, Nos. 1 & 2 (March & September 1999), p.49].

About minority rights

George Lobo states "The right of all citizens and groups must be safeguarded in any just society. It is highly desirable that minority rights are protected through constitutional means. Any violation of the rights of a minority is to be condemned." He states also that "the pastors of church do have the prophetic role of denouncing unjust structures and announcing by word and deed a new society that is marked by justice and love" (*Church and Social Justice*, pp.32, 33).

On Human Rights by Safdar Hasan Siddiqi

"The underlying spirit of every faith is that it provides an ethical and spiritual motivation to enable the individual to play a constructive role in building the society in a manner beneficial to all those living in it, irrespective of caste, colour or gender. All the prophets had a common message for the whole of humanity, not for any section of the human race. This message relates to the basic issue of human rights, the foremost being to bring an end to exploitation of man by man in any form—economic, social, political, religious or sectarian — and thus moving step by step towards the creation of a classless society. This goal can be achieved only if we treat all human beings as having equal rights and opportunities, and no discrimination is made between them on the basis of any bias" [*Christian Muslim Dialogue on Human Rights Solidarity* (ed.) by Mathews George Chunakara, Hong Kong: International Affairs — CCA, p.19].

About the right of girl child

Azim Sherwani writes, "A girl child is the first and foremost need of humanity because her survival is essential for the continuation of the species. To kill her means to kill coming generations. Denial of her right to live means denial of right to life to future generations. To honour her right to live amounts to honouring the right to life of future generations. But unfortunately, even this right is not provided to a girl child. All the studies in this connection have revealed that every measure is taken to eliminate the girl child by selective abortions and by female infanticide" (*The Girl Child in Crisis*, New Delhi: ISI, 1998, p.47).

Plight of girl children

According to Azim Sherwani "The newspaper reports of India testify the fact that girl children in the age group of 6 to 12 years have been victims of sexual abuse by the family members. Not only this, these reports also uncover the fact that small infants of even 2 to 5 years of age become victims of sexual violence—

rape by their own father, uncle or step-father. While researching on abortion, Meenakshi Apte discovered that most cases of teen-age pregnancies were incest victims" (*The Girl Child in Crisis,* p.86).

About tribal women

S.M. Michael comments: "The birth of a daughter was never regarded as a curse in a tribal family. The widows among the tribals were not helpless as those in caste society. She never gave up her feeling of independence and confidence. She hardly lamented over the widowhood. This position was possible because of her inborn virtues, viz. self-dependence, a spirit of confidence to carry on her livelihood, and above all, her right to re-marry and to lead a normal married life" ("Tribal culture and women's liberations", *Jeevadhara*, Vol. XXII, No.127, p.25).

Right to Constitutional Remedies

In case of violation of Fundamental Rights, there is a constitutional right to move the Supreme Court for appropriate remedies which can issue writs for the enforcement of the rights (Art. 32). Under Art. 224, a High Court can issue writs also for the redress of any other injury or illegality owing to the contravention of the ordinary laws. There are various forms of writs :

(1) *Habeas Corpus* (literally means "to have a body"). It is in the nature of the order calling upon the authority who has detained a person to produce the latter before the Court in order to let the Court know on what grounds he or she has been confined. The Court releases the person if there is no legal justification for the detention.

This is a powerful safeguard against arbitrary arrest or imprisonment.

(2) *Mandamus* (literally means "we command"). This commands the person to whom it is addressed to perform some public or quasi-public legal duty which he has refused to perform when the performance cannot be enforced by any other adequate legal remedy. It lies, not only against particular officers, but also against the Government itself.

(3) *Prohibition.* This writ is issued to an inferior court forbidding it to continue proceedings therein in excess of its jurisdiction. The idea is to compel inferior courts to keep themselves within the limits of their jurisdiction. This is available only against judicial or quasi-judicial authorities, and not against a public officer who is not vested with any judicial powers.

(4) *Certiorari* (literally "to be informed"). While "prohibition" is available during the pending of the proceedings, this writ can be used only after the order has been issued. It is used to quash an order or decision that is not properly made : (a) where the tribunal is not properly constituted; (b) where the subject matter of the enquiry is beyond the scope of the tribunal according to the law which created it; (c) where it assumed a jurisdiction on the basis of a wrong decision of facts; (d) where there has been a failure of natural justice or the decision has been obtained by fraud, collusion or corruption.

More recent decisions apply the writ also to administrative activities where natural justice has been violated by a party being not heard when the right of property or some other clear civil right of the individual is affected.

(5) *Quo Warranto* (literally "by what warrant"). This is a proceeding whereby the court enquiries into the legality of the claim a person asserts to a public office, and to oust him from its enjoyment if the claim is not well founded. It is based on the right of the public to see that an unlawful claimant does not usurp a public office.

Legal Aid to the Poor

(1) *Constitutional Provisions*. Free legal service to the poor is implicit in the Fundamental Rights to equality (Art. 14) and to life and liberty (Art. 21). Otherwise, the poor and the needy would be at a great disadvantage in obtaining justice. Now the 42nd Amendment Act, 1976, has made it a clear Directive Principle of State Policy (Art. 39A). It is for public spirited persons to see that it is implemented.

(2) *Legal Provisions*. Sec. 304 of the Criminal Procedure Code provides that if the accused has no sufficient means to engage a pleader, the Court must assign one for his defence at the expense of the Government.

Order 33 of the Code of Civil Procedure entitles an indigent person, who does not have sufficient means to pay court fees, to institute a suit, '*in forma pauperis*' without court fees. The person has to obtain permission of the Court to do so. He must apply for the permission with particulars regarding the suit and schedule of his assets.

Social action groups and voluntary organisations engaged in promoting social justice have a big role to play in enabling the poor to effectively make use of these rights.

The Government of India itself set up in 1980 a Committee for Implementing Legal Aid Schemes under the chairmanship of Justice P.N. Bhagwati, who has been doing pioneering work in bringing justice to the poor. The Committee was to formulate and implement a comprehensive legal aid programme, and to monitor schemes of legal aid in different States.

Some of the functions the Committee decided to assume are:

(a) to develop approapriate courses and reading material;
(b) to promote legal literacy among students of High Schools and Colleges;
(c) to coordinate the legal service programmes throughout the country;
(d) to set up Legal Aid Communication Cell in the All India Radio, Doordarshan and the Press Information Bureau;
(e) to conduct training programmes for para-legal workers;
(f) to organise services for lawyers for creating social justice awareness among them and sensitizing the legal profession to the demands of soical justice;
(g) to promote legal awareness among the weaker sections by every means possible;
(h) to organise legal aid camps in rural areas, slums and labour colonies;
(i) to promote public interest litigation;
(j) to conduct research and socio-legal surveys in the area of laws affecting the poor.

(3) *Public interest litigation.* Until the emergence of this possibility, the illiterate and underprivileged, could get no justice since no one else could take up their cases for lack of *locus standi*. In some recent judgments moved by Justice P.N. Bhagwati, the Supreme Court has enlarged the scope of *locus standi* to include any citizen who has the rightful concern to espouse the cause of the illiterate and underprivileged in the land. In some cases the Court has accepted just a letter from the victims of injustice, and converted the same into a writ petition.

Public Interest Litigation petitions can be filed in the Supreme Court under Art. 32 of the Constitution, or in the High Court under Art. 226 by public spirited persons like lawyers, social workers, journalists and voluntary organisations on behalf of the poor.

There have been some notable successes in cases like those of bonded labourers, undertrials in Bihar, and pavement dwellers in Bombay. The judgments may involve compensation to illegally detained persons, freedom from detention, stay of evictions and so on. When there is lack of sufficient evidence, the Court may appoint a Commission of experts to investigate the matter.

Public Interest Litigation has opened up new ways of obtaining justice for the poor. But the scheme has to be vigorously pursued at different levles. The majority of judges and lawyers do not seem to have been converted to the idea. So there could be inordinate delays and corruption could creep into the process. So there is need for great vigilance and use of this means in the context of popular movements and wider social action. Thereby, legislation in favour of slum dwellers, undertrials, unorganised labour, bonded labour, women, children and other weaker sections of the population could be implemented.

(4) *Speedy Justice*. There is need for reforming the whole legal system so that litigation is not too expensive and time consuming. The pernicious practice of adjourning hearings for little or no reason for the benefit of lawyers, must be stopped. Much of the colonial paraphernalia and formalities could be reduced without affecting the sanctity of the tribunals. Effective justice would be the best way of ensuring respect for the judiciary. It is natural that lawyers, like members of any other profession, wish to earn an adequate remuneration. But this should not be at the expense of the

poor. In the case of really needy clients, they should be ready to plead gratis or at reduced rates.

Legislation is not always necessary to resolve every legal problem. Often the result of court cases is loss of money, endless harassment and lasting animosities between the parties. As far as possible, disputes must be settled outside the court with the help of a conciliator. If a member of a Social Justice Cell were to bring the parties together to understand the legal implications of the case, including the expense and trouble it may cause, many would be inclined to compromise and find an out of court settlement. They would be free from machinations of lawyers to get people invloved in litigation by tendering wrong advice.

A new venture for the administration of speedy justice has developed in the form of *Lok Adalats* (People's Courts). Parties with disputes in an area are invited to come to a place to get them settled. They are helped by legal activists to compromise or follow the advice of the Lok Adalats.

This system existed traditionally in India in precolonial times in the form of *Nyaya Panchayats*. It still persists in some tribal and other village communites. Where it is already found, the legal activists should intervene only if there is need for government liaison or information on provisions of the law. This ancient practice should be revived and given legal status. The decisions of the Lok Adalats should also be given legal sanction. This will not happen unless public-spirited persons and organisations build up pressure through the mobilisation of the people themselves.

Ivory tower courts in far off towns and cities are beyond the reach of most villagers. When they do approach the courts, often the case is inordinately delayed. Hence the ponderous colonial legal system we have inherited needs to be radically modified to suit the needs of the poor, rural and slum people.

Mobile Courts with adequate number of magistrates, lawyers and social workers could visit different places on fixed dates and resolve the disputes of the people or help to resolve them. Mobile Courts were established in Delhi during the Emergency to book traffic offenders. There is no reason why such courts should not be instituted for the benefit of the weaker sections in far off places.

(The sections on 'Constitutional remedies' and 'Legal aid to the poor' are taken from George Lobo, *Human Rights in Indian Situation*, pp.61-65).

CONCLUSION

Human rights is a very significant issue which deals with human dignity and justice. In South Africa, Nelson Mandela and African National Congress challenged the apartheid and stood for the rights of the blacks. In North America Martin Luther King Jr. and Malcolm X. worked for the affirmation of the rights of the blacks. In Latin America, the struggle for human rights continued till the defeat of the colonizers. Even today in the context of globalization (which is another version of feudalism or capitalism), the marginated or the subalterns are undergoing severe crisis and their rights are not safeguarded. The western forces develop systems to help the dominant and not the poor. The resources they talk about are not meant to cater the needs of the down-trodden. There is an unholy nexus between the western elites and the dominant of the third world which work for oppressing and exploiting the poor. The MNCs and TNCs are for looting the resources from the third world and to destroy the systems developed by them. Their aim is to have monopoly over others, which is nothing but a new form of colonialism—neo-colonialism.

What is important is to identify the 'wolf' which tries to kill the 'lamb'. The first world agenda is to violate the human rights by all means. They use all tricks to win their goal. Unfortunately, several people support the agenda of the west without having a proper evaluation of the subject. One thing is very clear, those who are supporting the feudal systems do not belong to the Kingdom of God. They also cannot claim any solidarity with Jesus who sides the subalterns.

BIBLIOGRAPHY

Books

Abraham, K.C., *Eco-Justice: A New agenda for Christian Mission,* Bombay: BUILD, n.d.

Abraham, K.C., ed., *Cry for life,* Bangalore: SCM, 1993.

Antony, M.J., *Women's Rights,* Delhi, Hindi Pocket Books, 1996.

Antony, M.J., *Dalit Rights,* Delhi: ISI, 1998.

Castro, Fidel, *Tomorrow is too late,* Calcutta: National Book Agency, 1994.

Desrochers, John, *The Social Teaching of the Church,* Bangalore: C.S.C., 1982.

Durrany, K.S., *State Measures for the Welfare of Minorities,* Delhi: ISPCK, 1997.

Jaising, Indira, *Justice for woman,* Goa : The Other India Press, 1996.

Jesudoss, D.W., *Violence / Non-violence*, Madras : Gurukul, 1989.

Joseph, Annamma, ed., *Woman: Rights and Power,* Thiruvalla, Forum of Christian Workers for Women's Rights, 1998.

Just World Trust, *Human Wrongs,* Penang: Just World Trust, 1996.

Kudchedkar, Shirin & Sabrith Al-Issa, eds., *Violence against Women, Women against Violence,* Delhi: Pencraft International, 1998.

Lobo, George V., *Church and Social Justice,* Anand: Gujarat Sahitya Prakash, 1993.

Lobo, George V., *Human Rights: Indian Situation,* New Delhi, CBCI, 1991.

Manohar, Moses P., *Poverty and Human Rights,* Delhi: ISPCK, 1997.

Massey, James, *Roots,* Delhi: ISPCK, 1991.

Mathew, P.D., *Freedom of Religion and a "Debate" on Religious Conversion*, New Delhi: ISI, 1999.

Mathew, P.D. & Bakshi, P.M., *Ensuring a safe Environment: Laws against Pollution,* New Delhi: Indian Social Institute, 1993.

Mukhopadhyay, Swapna, ed., *In the name of Justice: Woman and law in society,* New Delhi: Institute of Social Studies Trust, 1998.

National Foundation for India, *The Unseen Worker: On the trial of the girl child,* New Delhi: Books for Change, 1998.

Pandey, J.N., *Constitutional law of India,* Allahabad: Central Law Agency, 1994.

Pereira, Winin, *Inhuman Rights,* Goa : The Other India Press, 1997.

Rajendran, Devadass S., *Humans Without Rights,* Madras: MMSSS, YMCA, 1989.

Shalini & Lathika, *Woman Soliciting Change,* New Delhi: ISI, 1998.

Shiri, Godwin, *The Plight of Christian dalits,* Bangalore: Asian Trading Corporation, 1997.

Webster, John C.B., *Religion and Dalit Liberation*, New Delhi: Manohar Publishers, 1999.

Zacheria, Mathai, ed., *Freedom of Religion in India,* Nagpur: NCCI, 1979.

Periodicals

Religion and Society, Vol. XXXVIII, Nos. 3 & 4 (Sept.-Dec. 1991).

Religion and Society Vol. XXXI, No. 1 (March 1984).

Journal of Tribal Studies, Vol. IV, No.1 (January-June, 2000).

Journal of Tribal Studies, Vol. IV, No.2 (July-December, 2000).

Religion and Society, Vol. XXIV, Nos. 243 (June–December, 1977).

Religion and Society, Vol. XXIX No. 2 (June 1982).

INDEX